# TOP SECRET FILE

Title...........The Goodies.........

---------------------------------

----------------File--------------

This book was produced by George Weidenfeld and Nicolson Ltd.
11 St. Johns Hill, London SW11
Copyright © Tim Brooke-Taylor, Graeme Garden & Bill Oddie, 1974
Designed by Anthony Cohen
ISBN 0 297 76816 6
Printed in Great Britain by Morrison & Gibb

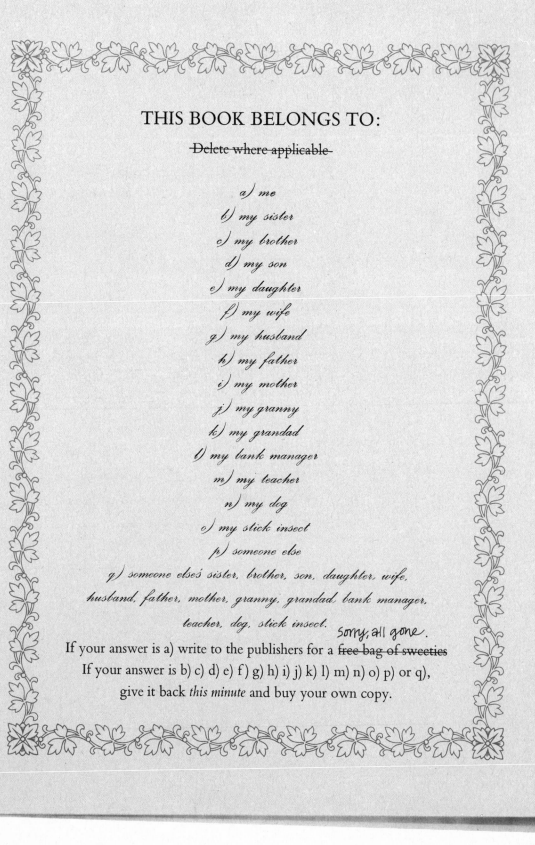

# THIS BOOK BELONGS TO:

~~Delete where applicable~~

a) me

b) my sister

c) my brother

d) my son

e) my daughter

f) my wife

g) my husband

h) my father

i) my mother

j) my granny

k) my grandad

l) my bank manager

m) my teacher

n) my dog

o) my stick insect

p) someone else

q) someone else's sister, brother, son, daughter, wife,
husband, father, mother, granny, grandad bank manager,
teacher, dog, stick insect. *Sorry, all gone.*

If your answer is a) write to the publishers for a ~~free bag of sweeties~~

If your answer is b) c) d) e) f) g) h) i) j) k) l) m) n) o) p) or q),

give it back *this minute* and buy your own copy.

## A Message from the Publishers

We believe that this is an important book.

The documents which go to make up *The Goodies File* were brought to us by Mrs Edna Tole, one-time employee of the men in question, and now seeking to reveal to the world the activities of the growing band of secret figures who even now move among us, operating 'without the law'.

We saw at once that what we had been given was 'hot stuff' —— as our American cousins have it — but we decided (bravely perhaps) to jolly well publish and be dashed!!

On reading the file, you may find it boring. More to the point, it *is* boring. Nevertheless, we felt that it was our duty to assist Mrs Tole in her ambition to expose the facts, and make a million pounds.

But let Mrs Edna Tole take up the story of how this book came to be...

---

397 Gallipoli Bldgs
Cherokee Way,
Cricklewood,
LONDON.

Saturday

Dear Readers,

Well, this is my first book, and I hope you all like it, tho' Norman's Janet says she is not sure, but then that's her for you.

Mr Widenfelt and Mr Nickolson have asked me to write a Forward, so here goes!!

I first entered the Goodies'es employment as long ago as two years ago, and since then have done for them three times a week. It was not ~~much~~ long before my suspicions were aroused regarding their activities, and I decided that enough is enough and someone must be told! Norman's Janet said no, but ...

Mrs Tole then goes on at some length to describe her painstaking, and often dangerous, researches — months spent sorting through waste-paper baskets, opening private letters, ransacking desks, reading diaries, and stealing things. She continues...

Blimey!!! I thought. I am holding in my hands a searing social document, as Mr Widenfelt was later to put it. Well then, I will expose the Goodies'es secrets to the world, and serve the ~~buggers~~ GOODIES right, specially not having let me have had a day off when Derek was taking me over to Crawley when Norman's Janet had the operation. Not that I care two hoots about

Eventually Mrs Tole goes on to describe how she was casually sacked by the Goodies for trying to film them in the bath, and how Norman's Janet got over the operation all right, but will never be the same again 'mark my words'.

That, briefly, is the story of how *The Goodies File* came to be put together by Mrs Edna Tole. And her reasons for doing it?...

...at least a million pounds but also to show the world that the so-called 'Goodies' (Goodies? Baddies more like) are no more than a bunch of lying, thieving, swivel-eyed, two-faced, ~~xxxxxxxxxx~~, lousy sons of

And our reasons for publishing the book?

Much the same as hers.

This file owes its existence to the unflinching hard work of a dedicated and courageous woman. If any of you should doubt her findings, or the accuracy of her testimony, let it be said that she came to us with impeccable references...

Mrs Edna Tole

# THE GOODIES

## No Fixed Abode, Nr. Cricklewood, London

To whom it may concern:

re: Mrs Edna Tole.

This woman is a good for nothing old rat-bag.

Yours

*The Goodies*

The Goodies

Mrs Tole first entered our employment as long ago as two years ago, and has proved an honest and hard-working cleaning lady, and we have got absolutely no complaints against ~~me~~ her.

Yours

Edna ~~~~ The Goodies   (Mrs)

This is true.

# THEIR SECRET LIFE!
## -BY EDNA TOLE (MRS)

I dont' know how you can bear
to look at these nasty pictures.
They shock me _every_ time!

Mr Bill relaxing with his "pets"

The three of them at
their "exclusive" club.

Mr Jim sharing a joke with a friend.

Coots!

WE DO
ANYTHING
ANY TIME

Author: Bill Oddie.

Printed by: Tatty & Cheap (Prunter)

# THE GOODIES ARE COMING...

# FOR YOU AND ANDYOU YOU!

This is their Brochure for sending to people. It is the only one they've got, but luckily everybody sends it straight back.

E.T. (mrs)

  PLEASE READ ON

'Help! – I need somebody

Help! – Not just any body'

The Beatles* (1967)

N THOSE WORDS Lennon and McCartney could so easily have been writing about the Goodies, but they weren't. In fact I've no idea *what* they were writing about half the time. All that rubbish about 'I am the Walrus' and Eleanor Rigby keeping her teeth in a jam jar or something, and *what* 'Lucy in the Sky with Diamonds' means I do NOT know! Still, it was better than the boring 'heavy' rubbish John's into these days or, indeed, those soppy tunes Paul sings now. Anyway – *Everybody* does need *Help* – sometime, somewhere – and The Goodies provide it – *Anytime, Anywhere*. So why not give us a call? – *Now!*

Well go on!

Oh alright then – we'll tell you *More*.

What do you get when you hire the Goodies?
Quite simply – us – three men (or two and a half) – minds, bodies, and socks – for you to do *whatever* you want with (as long as it doesn't tickle).

WARNING by H.M. Government
WINKING CAN DAMAGE
YOUR HEALTH

*
'The Beatles' were a popular singing group in the 1960s.
Now read on . . .

# WHO ARE THE GOODIES?

## TIMOTHY BROOKE-TAYLOR

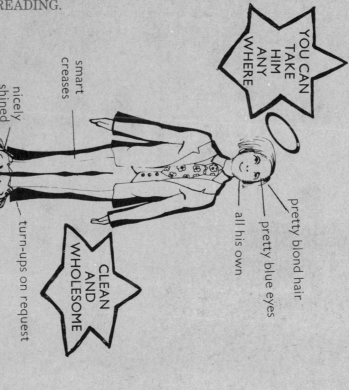

YOU CAN TAKE HIM ANY WHERE

pretty blond hair
pretty blue eyes
all his own
smart creases
nicely shined
turn-ups on request

CLEAN AND WHOLESOME

Born: Buxton, Derbyshire, 1940
Age: 23+
Height: Just right. Weight: Perfect.
Specialities:
Very good at making a speech (usually the same one). *Always* wears a tie (especially in the bath), has own suit, and speaks posh. Impersonates ladies (has own dresses, bras, knicks etc). *But* is nevertheless extremely Butch (considering he's so pretty). If you call at our office, Tim is the one who will speak nicely to you, shake your hand, lick your boots, etc, etc . . .

## DR. DAVID GRAEME GARDEN

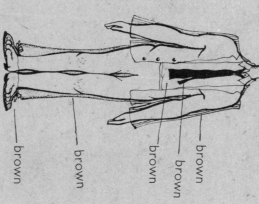
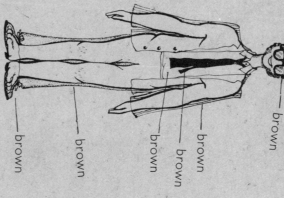
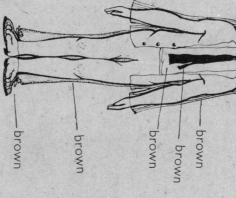
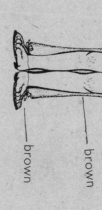

optional
brown
brown
brown
brown
brown
brown
brown

Born – (Invented), Scotland.
Age: Looks older than he is.
Height: The tallest. Weight: skinny.
Specialities:
Wears glasses, which means he is extremely clever and short-sighted. To be perfectly honest, he is a *Swot*. Will *Never* use one word when ten will be more confusing. When excited, jabbers like a Gibbon. All in all, if you want to blind anyone with science – Graeme's your man. Impersonates almost everybody, especially Eddie Waring. If you call at our office, Graeme is the one who will be so busy reading, he won't even notice.

## WILLIAM EDGAR ODDIE

greeny brown
purple
yellow
(makes you throw up- doesn't it!)
cream
(makes you throw up- doesn't it!)

RENT A SCRUFF

Born: Unfortunately, Rochdale, 1941.
Age: Work it out, if you *must* know.
Height: Not much. Weight: Variable.
Specialtities:
Difficult to single out any one of Bill's qualities – largely because he hasn't really got any. Used to be fat, and was very cozy to sit on. Now not so fat, but being sat on is still probably his best use. Very good at frightening people away. Also sings (which frightens people away). Hairy. Impersonates Old English Sheep dogs. If you call at our office Bill is the one who will bite your ankles. (For an extra fee he can be left..ocked up in his box.)

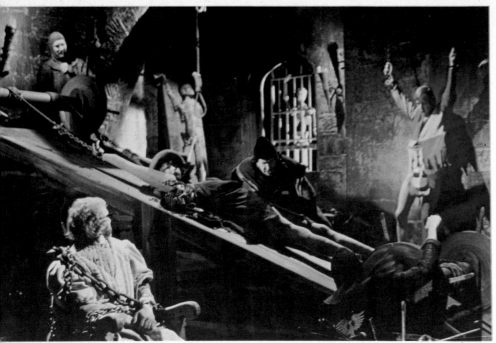

OUR CHOICE RE

"That *tort-ure* a lesson!" Here's Goody Oddie being cross examined (and he's cross alright) as he *racks* his brains to find a way out. But did Bill *crack*? No! Even though he stretched a bit! *Ouch!*

And here's The Goodies *jockee-ing* for position against the dreaded bagpipe spider – and they certainly taught him a *fling* or two!!

*N.B. THE GOODIES wish to thank the script-writer of "SCOOBY-DOO" for providing the captions on this page. THE GOODIES also wish to apologise for the picture of Tim's uncle, which has nothing to do with our past exploits, and has got in by mistake (even if it is quite funny).
N.N.B. Tim's uncle is available for children's parties, Bar Mitzvahs and "This is your Life" at a very reasonable hire-charge.

AST

UNIQUE

RD

Here's the answer! And how does this *grab* you Graeme? Yes, there's *machin-ations* afoot when the beastly bulldozers try to take over the world. But when those monster earth movers come up against The Goodies, well, it's a building *site* for sore eyes! Can you *dig* it?

But what's this? Tim *hanging* around on the job? Not likely, he's just *swinging* into battle, as usual. And his chums will soon get him off the *hook* . So what's he *up* to? We won't keep you in *suspense* any longer . . .

But, oh dear, Tim's certainly looking a little *cow'd* this time. Well, did you *heffer*?! Is he being taken for a *ride*? Or did he have no *udder* choice? Whoever *herd* of such a thing! In fact, here's the truth – and no more *bull* – it's not Tim at all, it's his loony uncle – better *steer* clear of *him*!

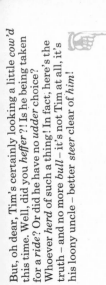

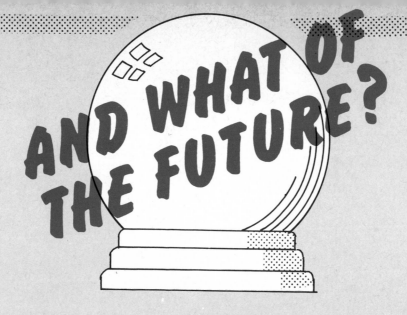

# AND WHAT OF THE FUTURE?

Already The Goodies have exiting NEW plans in the pipeline.
These are JUST A FEW of the thrilling endeavours they will attempt
during the coming year (probably).

Sailing around the World non-stop
(except to go to the lavatory) in
a dug-out Derby Ram

A Goodies health farm on the
Polar Ice Cap

The establishment of a brand new
Safari Park in the middle of
Trafalgar Square

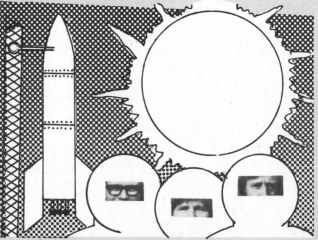

The first manned landing on the
Sun (leaving at night in case the
surface is too hot)

# What facilities can we offer? ? ?

If you hire **The Goodies** you get the benefit of the use of all these inclusive Goodies facilities – any MANY MORE (well, a few)

 **Door to Door Service – we get there Fast**  **Our Fully Mobile Office**

 **And the extensive Goodies Wardrobe**  **with its unequalled range of disguises – to suit any mission.**

# How Much Will It Cost?

We have always prided ourselves that we are cheaper than *Anyone Else* you will find *Anywhere*.

*We regret that, with the continued deterioration of the Country's economy, we have been forced to revise our fees a little this season. We trust you will not find the increases unreasonable.*

| | | |
|---|---|---|
| Consultation Fee: | ~~50p~~ | £10.00 |
| Personal Problems: | ~~50p~~ | £125.00 |
| Embarrassing Problems: | ~~£1.00~~ | £150.00 |
| Very Embarrasing Problems | ~~£1.25~~ | £250.00 |
| Very Difficult Problems: | ~~£0.75p~~ | £195.00 |
| Impossible Problems: | ~~£1.50p~~ | £10,000.00 |
| Mending Fuses: | ~~£0.02p~~ | £32.00 |

Prices do Not include VAT, tips, or danger money.

# How Do You Get In Touch With Us?

Just walk round the streets, wearing a Goodies T-shirt and waving a Goodies L.P. and shouting "Goodies For Ever!" – and we'll hear you eventually.

# Now – read what others say about The Goodies.

| ?? | •••• | NO | O O O | npq&2 |
|---|---|---|---|---|

'Which' Magazine

 "A rip off"
The Monkees

 "Fart oo nice"
M. Python

## TRY US – NOW!
## WE DO ANYTHING ANYTIME

**CONFIDENTIAL**

## H.M. DEPARTMENT OF NATIONAL SECURITY
### (and not Spying)

c/o MI9
13 Rotherfield Road
Welwyn Garden City
Herts.

*Top Secret*

*FIRST CLASS*

# HANDS OFF!!

TO:-

The Goodies,
No fixed Abode,
London NEI9 43CW

Dear Goodies,

Just a short note to thank you for clearing up that little matter involving
the Rt. Hon. ████████████ and the goats. Your efforts were greatly
appreciated by the Government, and by Her Majesty the ████ herself.
Jolly well done!

The bally Ruskies still don't know what hit them, and the CIA chaps are
fuming! My ankle is a lot better now, and I'll be up and about in no time,
though Doctor ████████ says the Prime ████████ will have to lay off the
cello for a week or two. The sideboard wasn't too badly burned, and it
turned out that Sister Maria Theresa had a wooden leg anyway, so no
harm done. Putting the old Concordre together again may take some time,
but at least the Blackpool Tower people aren't suing for damages - they
only lost the top bit anyway. ████████ sends his regards, and hopes to
see you when they take the bandages off.
Sorry about Tim's trousers.

All the best

~~████████████████████~~

Head of MI9

THIS LETTER IS <u>NOT</u> TO BE READ BY SPIES. PROMISE?

*found in Mr. Tim's desk*
*E. Tole (Mrs)*

# So...You think you're pretty naughty!?

## How do you measure up as a lover?

### Tick *your* answers to these questions, then turn to page 903 for your score

**1) When you see a girl, what do you look at first?**
a) Her eyes ✓
b) Her hair
c) Her teeth
d) Her Satinex Rubber Body-Stocking
e) Anything else

**2) What do you look at next?**
a) Her hands
b) Her nose
c) Your shoes ✓
d) Her husband

**3) If you want to date her, do you**
a) Ask her there and then
b) Phone her
c) Write a note
d) Forget about it ✓

**4) When you take her out on that oh-so-important first date, do you give her**
a) Flowers ✓
b) Chocolates
c) One

**5) Do you know where babies come from?**
a) Yes ✓
b) No
c) Not telling

**6) If you have a free evening, do you prefer to take out**
a) Your wife
b) Your secretary
c) A girl friend ✓
d) Your teeth

**7) What really turns you on?**
a) Being tickled
b) Tickling somebody else
c) Reading poetry ✓
d) Playing whist

**8) Are you *sure* you know where babies come from?**
a) Not telling ✓

**9) Do you use a deodorant?**
a) Yes ✓
b) No

Could have fooled me.

**10) Do you believe in holding hands before marriage?**
a) Yes
b) No

c) Don't understand the question ✓

**11) If you think you are in love with a girl of the opposite sex, do you**
a) Tell her so
b) Write poems
c) Run about with her in slow motion
d) Buy her a Satinex Rubber Body-Stocking ✓

**12) Do you realise how much a Satinex Rubber Body-Stocking costs!?**
a) No
b) Yes
c) Yes, but I know this little place ✓

**13) How many positions do you know?**
a) 1 ✓
b) 69
c) 1 *and* 69

**14) Do you consider yourself one of the world's greatest lovers?**
a) Yes ✓
b) Yes

**15) Are you sure?**
a) Well, possibly...
b) No, but you see...

**16) Answer Yes or No**
a) Yes
b) No
c) Well... ✓

**17) YES or NO!**
a) Yes ✓
b) No

**18) Do you honestly expect me to believe that?**
a) Yes! Yes! YES!!! No
b) Oh all right then, No ✓

**19) No. Exactly. In fact I put it to you that you are nothing more than a disgusting evil-minded little creep**
a) You cad!
b) I am undone! ✓

**20) Now answer carefully, when you go to bed at night do you**
a) Take a
b) Open y
c) Wear la

LIMITED EDITION

# The Goodies
## Garden of Verse

A compendium of youthful poetry by

*Tim Brooke-Taylor*    *Graeme Garden*    *Bill Oddie*

Collected and edited by

*Tim Brooke-Taylor*

With an introduction by

*Tim Brooke-Taylor*

Published by

*Soppy and Wet*

London

# INTRODUCTION

## BY

## TIM BROOKE-TAYLOR

*"From out the mouths of babes and sucklings*
*Cometh tears, and cometh chucklings.*
*And e'en from out thy childish lips*
*That lovesome thing — a poem — trips"*

TIM BROOKE-TAYLOR '74

*"Ruggish"*

ERIC MORECOMBE '44 & 6 MONTHS.

I HAVE ALWAYS BELIEVED that children write the best poetry – which goes to show what a fool I am. Yet, surely it is true that though, in our young years, we happily write poems every day, when we grow older, we suddenly stop. Why? Perhaps it is simply because any intelligent adult realises what a load of old cobblers it all is. Who knows? Certainly not me. And yet – is it truly foolish to cherish the fragrant innocence and joyful self-expression of youth? If 'tis, then happy I am to be a fool!

The following poems were all written during the authors' school years. It was not easy to collect the material together, spending painstaking months grovelling about in attics, rummaging down the backs of old settees and deciphering the walls of school lavatories. I would also like to acknowledge the co-operation of Bill's granny and the Metropolitan Police Obscenity Squad for allowing access to their 'Black Museum' (especially Bill's Granny's).

Tim Brooke-Taylor . . .

# ANIMALS

At The Zoo BY TIM BROOKE-TAYLOR, AGED 2

Someone's let the gibbon out, the gibbon's
                                got away
Oh isn't it a pity – that he's not here today
I did so want to see him – wherever can he be?
I wonder if he's hiding – shall I go and see?
I'm looking here, I'm looking there,
        I just can't find him anywhere
Where is he, where IS he?
            Where can that naughty gibbon be?
I'm looking high, looking low
Where is the little so and so.
If ever he comes back again –
I'll smash his rotten teeth in!

I Wish . . . BY TIM, AGED 20

I wish I was a dicky bird
Oh! wouldn't I be sweet?
I'd fly up to the apple tree
And sing tweet tweet tweet tweet
Tweet tweet tweet tweet tweet tweet tweet
Tweet tweet tweet tweet tweet tweet tweet
                            etc, etc . . .

Christopher Robin.

!!S??t! ???k!! Listen, who swears?
Christopher Robin has fallen down stairs.

Ode to 'The Tax Collector'.

Thirty five pounds 70.

Mice Pudding BY GRAEME GARDEN, AGED 12

Pies are nice
And so are mice.

My Dog        BY BILL ODDIE, AGED 4

I have a dog with seven paws
        With bloodshot eyes
        and savage jaws
        His teeth are long
        and pointed
        And his legs are
        double jointed
And he scratches hamsters eyes out with his claws.
He's got other nasty habits,
Like chewing bunny rabbits
And he often eats a pussy cat for tea.
If you say: "it isn't true!"
I'll set my dog on you.
And he'll bite your ruddy leg off – just you see!

Buffalo BY BILL ODDIE, AGED 8

Oh give me
a home
Where the
Buffalo roam,
And I'll show
you a house
With a very messy
carpet.

# L O V E

### AND OTHER POEMS

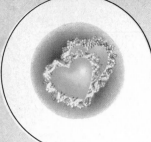
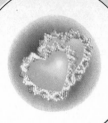

## The Kiss BY TIM BROOKE-TAYLOR, AGED 9

Linda Cosgrave kissed me!
It nearly made me sick
I wasn't even looking –
Oo what a beastly trick!
Her mouth was wet and greasy
And her sticky little lips
Were full of salt and vinegar –
She'd been eating fish and chips.
I told her she was "yucky",
And she went off in a huff.
If that's what kissing girls is like,
I'm going to be a puff!

## SATIRE Our Leader
### BY GRAEME GARDEN

William Gladstone –
What a squirt.
He wears lipstick
and a skirt.

## Trousis BY GRAEME GARDEN, AGED 31

Always wear trousis
In Public Houses,
Or you'll have nowhere to put the change.

## Blank Verse.
### BY TIM BROOKE-TAYLOR, AGED 9

## Love Is BY BILL ODDIE, AGED 16

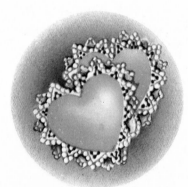

There's a girl in 3C
With a wart on her knee
And a pimple upon her behind.
I gave her 3p
And she showed it to me
Don't you think that was awfully kind?
P.S. Wonder what she'd do for a quid!

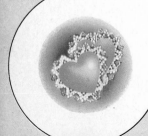
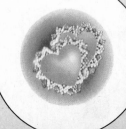

**|2|**

*No time to lose!   Still time to win!*

*hurry! hurry!   hurry! hurry!   hurry! hurry!   hurry! hurry!*

Lucky Number: **254**

Dear **Graeme**

Great News!

You, **Graeme**     may already be one of the lucky winners in this year's grand
Nobel Prize draw!

Yes, your number may be the lucky one which could already have won you,
**Graeme**     one of the few coveted Nobel prizes!

All you need to do is send in your enclosed lucky number, and you
could receive a Nobel Prize by return of post:

The envy of all your friends, and an elegant addition to your
living room wall or mantelpiece, and an exciting talking point
at all the parties you hold at **no fixed abode**

Just send in your lucky number, and answer these simple questions:—

1)  Identify three discrepancies in Einstein's special theory of Relativity
    with special reference to the constant $3x/c$.

2)  Define the place of Molecular Biology in a clone community.

3)  Complete the following sentence:—

    "I think I should have a Nobel Prize because

Good luck!      Yours   *Ron Jones.*

(This competition is not open to employees of the Nobel Dynamite Co. Ltd.,
or members of their families.)

*Boots, Boots, Boots, Boots, Marchinup & Downagain,*
*Solicitors and Commissioners for Oaths.*

*'Bertfreda',*
*19 Mohammed Alley,*
*Gosport,*
*Hants.*

The Goodies
No fixed abode
Near Crouch End

Date as postmark

Dear Sirs

I have been instructed by my client to communicate with you regarding the alleged events, beginning Sunday February 16th.  The aforementioned events, as you will recall, were as follows:-

1.    On the evening in question, you did unlawfully gain entrance to my client's premises by impersonating a six-legged pantomime Dromedary with a silly French accent.  As such, you were accepted, in good faith, as a guest in my client's house, and even given a cup of tea and fifteen Bakewell tarts in a nose-bag.

2.    My client, (hereinafter referred to as 'my client') had to leave the room for a moment for urgent consultation with his business associate, the Rev. 'Kinks' Codd.

3.    While he was out of the room, you ate the piano.

4.    On his return, my client (in a tolerant mood as he has no great taste for music) requested an explanation.  He was immediately set upon by you, without provocation, resulting in a wilful breach of his trousers.

5.    You then proceeded to ridicule my client (hereinafter referred to as 'old skinnypins'.)

6.    This behaviour continued for some five or six months, until last August, when it was brought to my client's notice that a six-legged pantomime Dromedary, <u>wearing his hat</u>, had attempted to cash a cheque for £250,000 in his name at the local off-licence.  This aroused his suspicion.

7.    On September 2nd, choosing his moment, my client informed you of his misgivings, and requested an explanation.

8.    You ate his undergarments.  (Mauve.)

9.    My client, reasonably in the circumstances, requested you to leave his premises, which you refused to do, even when threatened with eviction.  You further claimed 'Squatters' Rights' in his home, and applied for arbitration to the Rent Tribunal.

P.T.O.

10. My client has subsequently agreed to pay you £13 a week rent.

11. On September 23rd, my client called in the Bailiffs.

12. On September 24th the Bailiffs arrived. You joined them in a rather amusing routine which involved papering the parlour.

13. The Rev. 'Kinks' Codd was obliged to intervene on my client's behalf.

14. He was papered.

15. During the month of October, my client was obliged to be away from home during his stay at the 'Bide-a-wee' Funny Farm, Okehampton.

16. On his return, he discovered you still in residence, but was prepared to accept your explanation that you were not the same pantomime Dromedary, but that you were in fact the late Sarah Bernhardt.

17. My client's amateur production of 'My Fair Lady' at the Godalming Occasional Players Theatre, Wolverhampton, on October 3rd, was universally hailed as a disaster on the first night. And I quote ".... the role of Eliza Dolittle was played by the late Sarah Bernhardt like a six-legged pantomime Dromedary with a silly French accent .... (the Wolverhampton Courier)."

18. October 4th: my client consulted us to seek legal advice.

19. October 5th: we sent my client a bill for our services.

20. October 6th: the bill was paid by my client.

21. October 7th: we lost interest in the case.

And so, for the moment, the matter rests. However my client has expressed some concern regarding the current situation, and informs us that it has had some considerable effect on his previous relationship with Miss Desiree Gaspinforit (formerly the Rev 'Kinks' Codd.)

Charges are not to be pressed by us, but we look forward to your early reply regarding just compensation.

Yours

*Geronimo Boots*

(pp Boots Boots Boots Boots Marchinup & Downagain.)


PS - Will you please get off my desk?

# THE GOODIES

## No Fixed Abode, Nr. Cricklewood, London

Dear Mr. Boots,

        In reply to your letter:

1) We deny all knowledge of the events mentioned.

2) We have <u>never</u> dressed up as a pantomime dromedary - with or without a silly accent.

3) It must have been three other people - possibly the Beverly Sisters, or even the Swedish Prime Minister and two like minded friends.

4) Alternatively, have you considered the possibility that it may not have been three people in a skin, but might actually have been a real pantomime dromedary?

5) We have no intention of paying compensation.

6) and, sixthly,

7) Your client, who is known to us, should stop telling fibs and return immediately to his husband, last heard of on a camping holiday in Harlow New Town.


Your Obedient Servants,

*The Goodies*

following the
a bunch of swine -
this particular time has come circumstances of
be in default of my trouser and await also our client's instructions.
ovisions will be taken to see it done if we do not ---  you will

*Geronimo Boots*
*oh, all right forget it.*

Geronimo Boots

**METROPOLITAN POL**

BCK

Dear Mrs. Tole, (Mrs.)

Thankyou for your most <u>interesting</u> letter. The information you enclosed suggests that this case might well provide for me the promotion I so richly deserve, and for you the ~~sum of one million pounds~~ satisfaction of a job well done.

However, I think we shall need more concrete evidence. I enclose half a brick, and I should be grateful if you would "plant" it. Then — I shall <u>pounce</u>!

Don't forget though, as we say in the force — 'Softly Softly, catchee monkey!'

Yours.

P.C. Bent (P.C.)

many thanks! ~~Let~~ have planted the half-brick you so far nothing has come up — despite plenty of watering and manure. However, we must wait and see. But now the good news, I <u>have</u> caught a monkey,

P.T.O.

# METROPOLITAN POLICE—CRIMINAL RECORDS DEPARTMENT

Name of Villain or Tearaway    Oddie, Bill

Name (in the right order)    Bill Oddie

Date of birth: ?

Age: 30⅛

Sex: Male

Height: 3 ft. 6¼"

Colouring: Hair the colour of Jacobean stained oak. Eyes - mouse

Inside Leg: Practically none.

Mug Shots:

Educasion: Mother Goose Infant Primary (Godalming)
(Expelled for cheating.)
Mother Goose Approved Infant Primary (Isle of Wight)
Open University (Escaped.)

Known Activities: Member of notorious Goodies mob.
Believed to have been involved in 'The Case of the Chinese Box' (by Dorothy L. Sayers, £1.50p., Victor Gollancz).
Fell ~~off~~ ~~like~~ back of like in June 1971. Subsequently phoned on 'Police 5'.
Sings:
Not much on this one I'm afraid - but we'll keep trying. (Characteristic habit, when nervous, of lightly drumming his head against policemen.)

Personally, I don't think it's what it's cracked up to be, but that's only my opinion. P.C. Bent.

Other Information:

Alias: Fungus Face, Fuzzy peg, or William Oadie

Dabs:

# METROPOLITAN POLICE—CRIMINAL RECORDS DEPARTMENT

Name of Villain or Tearaway  Brooke - Taylor - Tim

Name (in the right order)  Taylor - Tim   Taylor - Tim - Brooke   Tim Taylor   Tim - Brooke
Brooke - Tim   Taylor

Date of birth: August 17  1893

Age: 21

Sex: ● ● ● ● (the more blobs the better)

Height: 10 st. 5 lb.

Colouring: NONE

Inside Leg: Curiously appealing

Mug Shots:

Educasion: Mother Goose Infant Primary (Godalming)
I. Canem's Academy for the sons of gentlefolk with funny names.
The University of Life (Failed)
Public School - Winchester ('73)

Known Activities: Crochet & Needlework (has won prizes)
Member of notorious Goodies mob since 1970.
Known sympathiser with Old Age Pensioners.
Alias - Jack the lad
Sten-gun Steve
Hopalong Wilkinson R.N. (Ret.a.)
Winnie the Pooh.
Pooh the Winnie.
P.C. Bent.
Gladys Hasbottle
His Holiness Pope Pius II
Abdul al Rahman and his educated Dromedary.

Other Information:

Henry VIII died in 1547.

this is true. P.C. Bent.

Dabs:

# METROPOLITAN POLICE—CRIMINAL RECORDS DEPARTMENT

Name of Villain or Tearaway     Garden, Graeme

Name (in the right order)     Graeme Garden

Date of birth: Feb. 18th 1943

Age: 116     73   73
            43  -43
            116  30

Sex: ✓

Height: Average

Colouring: Average

Inside Leg: Average

Mug Shots:

Educasion: Mother Goose Infant Primary (Kirkcudbright)
~~Eton, Harrow~~ Penge.
Universities: Cambridge, Oxford, Harvard, Yale,
St. Andrews, Sussex, Solihull Poly.

Qualifications: MA., M.B., B.Chir, D.Ph., Ph.D., Dh.P., L.h.B., L.O.O.

Known Activities:     Member of Goodies Mob.
NOT
│ Known as 'Brains'.
Picked up for questioning last April, and asked us many
                                        interesting questions
Arrested while in possession of £3,000,000 pounds in gold bull
and charged with possessing £3,000,000 pounds in gold bull
(acquitted).
Parking offence!
Charged with riding a bike without lights. (aged 3)
Personally, I myself brought him in last week - drunk and
disorderly. But when I sobered up, he'd gone. Sorry.

Other Information:

THIS MAN IS ~~DGA~~ ~~DANJERU~~ ~~DANGEROUS~~ ~~DANGUEROS~~ DANGEROUS[US] SAFE.

Dabs:

Sorry — some of
the dabs are mine.
Sorry. P.C. Bart.
(sorry)

**METROLOPITAN POLICE**
**IQ TEST**

*This will give you some idea of P.c. Bent's calibre! E.T. (Mrs)*

Name   P. C. Bent

**1. What is the next number in this sequence?**

1  2  3  4  5  6...?

*123, 457*

**2. A = 1**
**B = 2**
**C = ?**            *C*

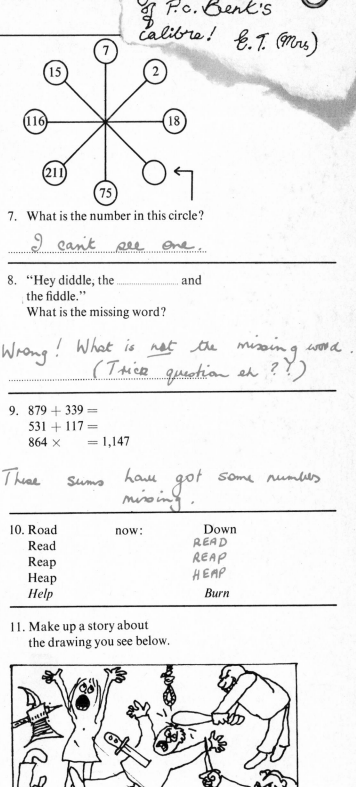

**7. What is the number in this circle?**

*I can't see one.*

**3. Which is the odd man out?**

*Chief Inspector 'Nancy' Bottle*

**8. "Hey diddle, the _____ and the fiddle."**
**What is the missing word?**

*Wrong! What is not the missing word.*
*(Trick question eh ?!)*

**4. Bread is to butter as knife is to** *cut it with*

**9.  879 + 339 =**
**531 + 117 =**
**864 ×     = 1,147**

*These sums have got some numbers missing.*

**5. What have all these shapes in common?**

□  ○  △

*They are all in question 5)*

| 10. Road | now: | Down |
|---|---|---|
| Read | | READ |
| Reap | | REAP |
| Heap | | HEAP |
| *Help* | | *Burn* |

**11. Make up a story about the drawing you see below.**

**6. What does this remind you of?**

*A Rorschack ink-blot test.*

*One bright morning Milly Molly Mandy set off shopping. "Come on you lot" she*
*P.T.O*

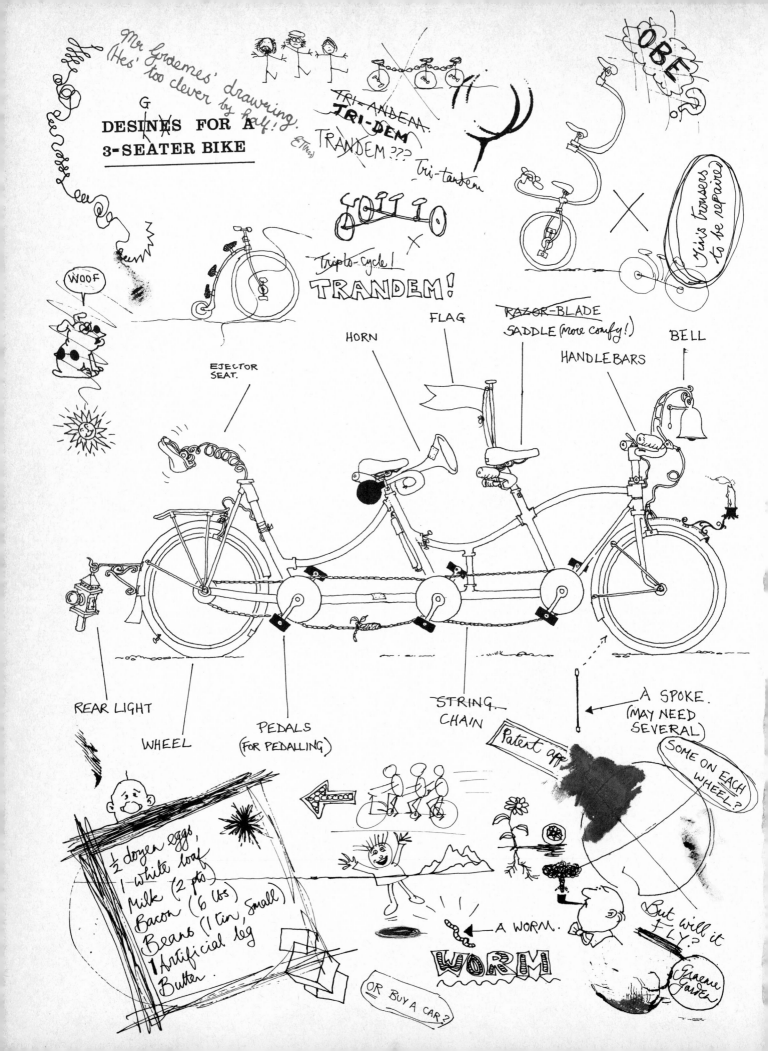

# COOKERY CORNER

## How To Cook A Leather Armchair.

① PEEL CAREFULLY

② Remove springs.....

as always; keep springs for making **soup**

③ Simmer gently in 75 gallons of french otter grease for 36 years, or until tender.

④ ADD onions, shallots, parsley, and any left-over armadillo giblets...

CHUCK IT OUT.

⑧ ADD cushions, and garnish with live toads.

add salt to taste

⑦ open a window.

⑤ GENTLY stir in ½ pint of cream, or if you have no cream 17¼ poodles' eyes...

⑥ allow to stand until offensive

**1** ST STEP : Imagine you are sweeping the ballroom. Sweep to the left – then to the right.

Count: 1 2 3 4 1 2 3 4 1½

# THE G

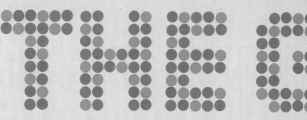

Here demonstrated by Norman and Norma Higginbottom – a bank-clerk and a hair-stylist – from Esher (actually it's Graeme and Tim dressed up – hoo hoo!)

## THE GOODY – THE DANCE T

**2** ND STEP : It's as if you have found a lighted cigarette on the floor – you stamp your foot on it to put it out.

Count: 1 2 3 4 5 6 7 8 ⅓

**4** TH STEP : Now – as if holding your foot in your hands you hop 2 to the right – count 1 2 3 4, 2 to the left – count 5 6 7 8 – twice round the room. Count: 9 10 11 12 13 etc. to 119 – hop backwards – Count: 119, 120, Forwards 121 – 122 and fall flat on your back.

**3** RD STEP : BUT – it burns a hole right through the sole of your shoe and you leap in the air.

Count: 9–10

**5** TH STEP : Help your partner up. Count 1 – 2. And – as if by accident – pull her over backwards. Count: 3 4

C'MON EVERYBODY – TAKE YOUR PARTNERS

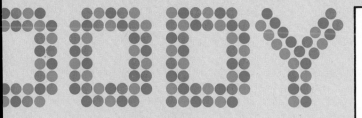

**IT'S NEW
IT'S GROOVY
IT'S AMAZINGLY
COMPLICATED**

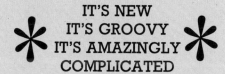

## S SWEEPING THE BALLROOM

**8** TH STEP : Grab her in a double leg-lock with a back arm twist.

Count : 5 6 7 8

**6** TH STEP : Next – kick your partner in the stomach, whilst shouting out "Clumsy git!"

Count : 1 2

**9** TH STEP : Give her a playful karate flip arm twisting neck bender – Whee !

Count : 9-10          OUT !

**7** TH STEP : Let her kick you back.

Count : 3 4

**10** TH STEP : Phone for a) a masseur, b) an ambulance, c) an undertaker, depending on the damage inflicted. Give yourself as LONG AS YOU NEED to recover. ORFT YOU GO AGAIN Same movements for 2nd verse – only man dances lady's steps

IT'S
AS SIMPLE
AS
THAT.

## N THE FLOOR – AND DO THE GOODY – WOW!

# HOW TO PLAY
# 'Land of Hope and Glory'
## on milk bottles

by Tim Brooke-Taylor

Most of us like to play 'Land of Hope and Glory' at least three or four times a day. However, if there isn't a gramophone, or musical instrument handy, I find a satisfactory rendering can be achieved by filling 6 milk bottles to the levels indicated below, and producing the required notes by striking them with a piano or gramophone. Or even a ruler. Thus

| 1 | 2 | 3 | 4 | 5 | 6 |
|---|---|---|---|---|---|
|   | 1" | 2" | 3" | 4" | 5" |

| Land | of | hope | and | glory, | mother | of the | free |
|------|-----|------|-----|--------|--------|--------|------|
| 5 | 5 | 3-4 | 5 | 4-3 | 2-2 | 1-2-3 | 1 |

Some of those involved!
as snapped by me.
(Edna Tole) (Mrs.)

"The Goodies" (1/60 sec, f11.)

Mr. Tim. (10 sec. time exp. f 22)

Mr. Bill (arrowed). (Pentax Brownie. 135mm lens.)
5.6 secs. f 1/30 Agfacolor.

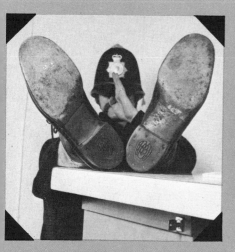

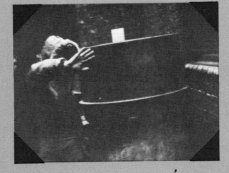

'Autumn Nocturne' by E. Tole (Mrs)
(courtesy Radio Times Hulton
Picture Library.)

P/c Bent ( 👫 🌦 )

Mr. Graeme ( 1/200 flash
+ cloud filter.)

Chief Inspector George W. Bottle.
(indoor flash)

WORDS & MUSIC BY
BILL ODDIE.
with help from Tim.
and Graeme

# GOODIES THEME SONG

GOODIES - GOODY GOODY GUM DROPS   Don't like Gum drops (T)
How about LIQUORICE ALLSORTS ?! (Graeme)
BUM BUM too rude!   TUM TUM even ruder   YUM YUM ✓

TAKE A LITTLE GOOD ADVICE   Take a little lovely TRAM   PARADISE ?
TAKE A TRIP TO BOGNOR REGIS
Doesn't rhyme - How about WEST HAM ?   rhymes / Blackburn Rovers

IT'S REALLY NOT SO HARD TO FIND
YOU'VE GOT IT IN YOUR HEAD FOOT HAND MIND ✓

IT'S WHATEVER TURNS YOU ON ← Is this a drugs reference? No! Pity.

GOODIES   GOODIES   Why?   It's whatever turns you on - get it?   No - GOODIES
SWITCH   SWITCH

IT'S ANYTHING YOU WANT IT TO BE
To rhyme with BE please!
A suggestions?   OR A   PolarBear   suggestions?
A WOMBAT
Radioactive isotope?   RECORD   Okapi   Lady's KNEE   the BBC   fee gee   cup of tea wee   O.B.E ✓

A CIRCUS OR A SEASIDE PIER   PEER   HAPPEN
WE MAKE IT EVER SO NEAR VERY QUEER   bear dear   HERE.

FINE FOR EVER-Y BOD-Y   YOU-OO-OO- AND ME - what about me?
All THE FAMILY ?   X rubbish !

GOODIES   GOODIES   All THE FAMILY

GOODIES - GOODY GOODY GUM DROPS   AAAAH OO OO   Yeah Baby!
GOODIES - GOODY GOODY GUM DROPS   BUM BUM TUM TUM   YUM YUM TOO MUCH
Liquorice Allsorts   BUM BUM TUM TUM   YUM YUM Far Out!
WE'RE COMING FOR YOU OW EEK   UH !
Liquorice Allsorts

No we're not.

ANYONE CAN RIDE ALONG - WE ARE VERY BIG & STRONG
THERE'S NOTHING THAT YOU CANNOT DO.   ANYONE CAN SING OUR SONG.
AND YOU'LL BE A GOODY DOO TOO TOO TOO 2.   Who'd want to?
ALL YOU NEED'S A LITTLE LOVE - me?   GOODIES - GOODY GOODY GUM DROPS etc
BUM BUM TUM TUM YUM YUM

*The Goodies*

*Annual Prize-Giving Dinner*

Your presence is requested at a slap-up feed
at the
HOTEL DE POSH

**Dress**  Goodies' T-shirts and dirty jeans
Anyone wearing a tie will be thrown out

**Bring Bottle
and Raquel Welsh**

# ORDER OF EVENTS

**7.30 Dinner**

## Menu

*Salt and Vinegar crisps or Scotch Broth with enormous dumplings*

*Eggs with Soldiers*

*or*

*Fishfingers and Baked Beans*

*or*

*Chip Butties*

*or*

*All the above, served on one plate with lots of tomato ketchup*

*Christmas Cake with N O Marzipan*

*Pop*

*Marshmallows you can pick the chocolate off*
*Mars Bars (to be sucked not bitten)*
*Sherbet Fountains*

*Custard Pies (not to be eaten at all)*

**7.40 Second Helping**

**7.45 More Pudding**

*Lucozade with Sugar in it*

**7.46 More 'Pop'**

*or*

**7.47 Community Burping**

*More 'Pop'*

**7.49 Speeches**

**7.49 & 20 seconds End of Speeches**

**7.50 The Goodies Awards — Prize Giving**

Announcement of Winners by your Master of Ceremonies Mr. Eddie Waring
Followed by explanation of announcements by Richard Baker

## THE GOODIES AWARDS
(Three Nominations in each Category)

### *For Falling Over Better Than We Do*

**Nominations:** Charlie Chaplin  *107th*
Michael (Crawford) — *1st*
Rodney Marsh  *2nd*

### *For Being Very Fancy-Able*

*2nd 3rd 4th 5th 6th 7th 8th
9th 10th 11th 12th*

**Nominations:** Half the Young Generation
*1st* (Jane Fonda)
The other Half of the Young Generation

*Awarded Tim's Prize!*

### *For Making Us Laugh*

**Nominations:** Tony Blackburn  *Disqualified.*
The Government's Economic Policy
(Morecambe) and Wise

*1ST AGAIN!*

*Awarded special prize 3 £5 for a good try.*

## THE PRIZES
presented by the President of the United States

Mr *David Frost*  (name not certain at time of printing)

**8.30 Cabaret** Starring: Tommy Cooper, Rod Hull & his Emu, Randy Newman,
Paul Simon, The Band, Tom & Jerry and Buster Keaton
(Three hours of recently discovered film comedy masterpieces)

(Des O'Connor & Engelbert Humperdink have kindly agreed not to appear)

**12.30 Dancing** with Pan's People To the music of The Beatles (special farewell performance)

**Three Days Later**  *Never did turn up!* —— **The Queen**

POWDER PUFF

WIG

EYELASHES

VERY VERY SILLY HAT

TIM

SHOULDER-PADS

SUIT

IN CASE OF SUN

O.B.E.

CORSET

SENSIBLE SHOES

BULLET-PROOF HANKIE

PORTABLE GRAMOPHONE FOR 'LAND OF HOPE & GLORY'

HAT

MICROPHONE

AMPLIFIER

SACK

AFTER-SHAVE

BOXING GLOVES

DISGUISE

KNUCKLE-DUSTERS

SCISSORS

STICKING PLASTER

IN CASE OF DEEP SNOW

BILL

TASTEFUL TROUSERS

OLD SCHOOL TIE

BOVVER PLIMSOLLS

COMFY PULLOVER

Graeme was a proper swanky-boots!

Well you could see that Mister Bill was bound to be a bad-un!

# KleenoSmalls Laundry Limited

CLIENT ..... *The Goodies* .....................................................

| ITEM | NO. | CHECK | £ | p |
|---|---|---|---|---|
| Dirty Vests | 3 | ✓ | | ·60 |
| Pants | 3 prs | ✓ | | ·60 |
| Hankies | 3 | ✓ | 15 | ·05 |
| Shirts | 2 | ✓ | | ·75 |
| Goodies T-shirt | 1 | ✓ | | ·75 |
| Leopard-skin body stocking + hat | none | ✗ | 12 | ·43 |
| Brown trousers (Tim's) | 1 pr | ✓ | 1 | ·00 |
| Clean Vests | 6 doz | ✓ | | ·60 |
| Eggs | 1 doz | ✓ | 2 | ·00 |
| 6 legged pantomime dromedary skin | 15 | ✗ ✓ | | ·02 |
| Funny clothes - various (Bill's) | 1 | ✓ | 74 | ·04 |
| Tights | 1 pr | ✓ | | ·12 |
| Hot air balloon - (stained) | 1 | ✓ | | ·12 |
| Bra | 1 | ? | | ·12 |
| Aprons | 317 | ✓ | 317 | ·00 |
| Y-Front Hovercraft (small) | 1 | ✓ | | ·50 |
| more aprons | 2 | ✗ | 2 | ·00 |
| Suede safari boots | ½ pr | ✓ | | ·00½ |
| Sausage, bacon, beans, chips + egg | | | | |
| (sunny side up) | twice | | 1 | ·20 |
| | | (+ VAT) | £28,431 | 73 p |

PAID
15 MAR 1974

No Liability accepted for Belts, Buckles, Buttons, String, Suspenders or Zips

# GOODIES' TOP SECRET FILE

**Title** THE RISE AND FALL *and rise* OF THE GOODIES

FEB 1st – FEB 12th 1974

THE GOODIES
SING SONGS FROM
THE GOODIES

DECCA

## GOODIES SPLIT

blues ', with
tasty guitar
Francis of
lapton?) – in
iness'' (Bill
ne of THE
ues lyrics

n damn

soul.
ay night

and Roll.''

it like it is!
n amazing
at explodes
gins'' with
nes Brown
of; whilst
'' is pure
'Wolsey''
doing a
nd all, I

hours;
The
ellent

The savage ups and downs of the pop rat-race have claimed three more victims. It was revealed today that the apparently oh-so-successful-would-be-chart-busters – THE GOODIES – have, in fact decided to break up. BILL ODDIE, musical spokesman for the group, said: "We feel that commercial demands are incompatible with our artistic integrity". Tim Brooke-Taylor elaborated on the statement: "We're skint!" he said. When asked "why?", he suggested "Probably it's because we're such rotten singers". He then burst into tears. Rumours that Graeme Garden is going to go solo were described by the others as ****ing ridiculous.

# THE GOODIES

## No Fixed Abode, Nr. Cricklewood, London

THIS MINUTE BOOK BELONGS TO:

THE GOODIES

Minutes of a Special Emergency Meeting

A special emergency committee meeting was held outside the
Cricklewood Labour Exchange at 10.15 am on Monday 16th June.
Tim Brooke-Taylor was in the chair, Graeme Garden was on the
pavement, and Bill Oddie was grovelling in a nearby dustbin.
The main item under discussion was the grave economic crisis
brought about by the recently reported bankruptcy of the Goodies
Pop Group. The treasurer was asked to present his financial
report which is here attached.

He the there was an ~~old~~                                    obblers
we stung on t'                                                  ubbish
eas hu                                                             elf
How it                                                            l in
Tim Se                                                            old
fat el                                                           lory

BM who ri                                                         up
trash a                                                           it
11 -r                                                            and
we a

In r                                                            re.

Dear
toda                                                            st
two                                                            n't
had

On the                                             as closer to you,
felt the                                              intensity than
earlier                                             in the Grunewald.

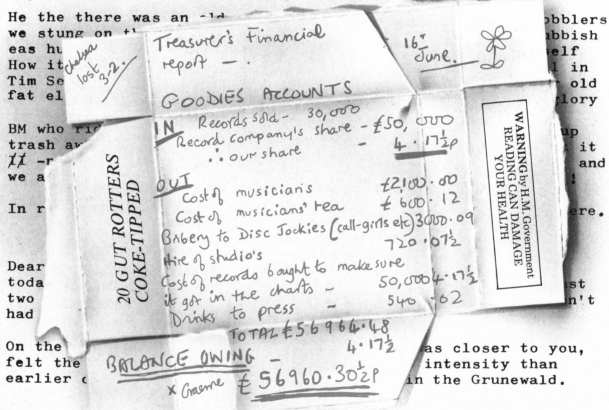

Treasurer's Financial report —.    16ᵀ June.

Chelsea lost 3-2.

**GOODIES ACCOUNTS**

**IN**
Records sold - 30,000
Record company's share - £50,000
∴ our share - 4.17½p

**OUT**
Cost of musicians                          £2,100.00
Cost of musicians' tea                     £600.12
Bribery to Disc Jockeys (call-girls etc) 3000.09
Hire of studio's                           720.07½
Cost of records bought to make sure
it got in the charts -          50,000  4.17½
Drinks to press -                  540 .62

TOTAL £56 964.48
                 4.17½

**BALANCE OWING** -
x Graeme  £ 56 960.30½ 2P

20 GUT ROTTERS COKE-TIPPED

WARNING by H.M. Government READING CAN DAMAGE YOUR HEALTH

                  chairman then tabled the motion
The ~~committee has therefore decided~~ that we should sign on
with a big powerful agent/manager and have another go.

Motion carried by unanimously with two ~~abstens~~

                                        ~~abstain~~

                            not voting

                            T B T

**Izzy Bent Management Limited**
**Pop Agent**
**(Affiliated to The the Low Grade Organisation)**

Dear Boys already,

How pleased I was to get your letter oyvay! ~~Love~~ your singing! (MUST hear you sometime) Sure, I'd be delighted to ~~bleed you dry~~ represent you. You wanna be stars? No bother, my sons! No sooner said than fiddled. Please sign & return enclosed contract already (enclosing blank cheque) and we'll fix up a meeting.

Love Izzy

---

**Rookem, Screwem and Scarper, (Solicitors),**
**Queer Street, London W2.**

*Illegal yet binding contract*

1. The said ....Goodies.... shall be the exclusive property of the said Izzy Bent for a period of five hundred years or life (whichever is the longer)

2. All earnings of the ....Goodies.... shall be divided in the proportion of ..50/50..

3. The said Izzy Bent reserves the right to terminate this contract and nip off to ..the Bahamas.. He must, however, give due and fair warning of this intention.

Signed: (for Izzy Bent) ..Izzy Bent..
(for the Goodies) Graeme Garden Bill (Oddie)
Tim Brooke-Taylor

*Notes*

1. ....Goodies.... herein taken to mean T. Brooke-Taylor, G. Garden & B. Oddie or anyone with similar names; their friends, family, children of the next ten generations, dogs, stick insects etc. etc. ....

2. ..50/50.. ie. ..50p.. to ..The Goodies.. and ..£50.. to ..Izzy Bent..

3. "Due and fair warning" shall mean ..3-5 seconds..

*The small print*

BUCKINGHAM PALACE, LONDON SW1, ENGLAND

Dear Boys already
    Thanks for the cheque.
Sorry - can't make meeting just now - am
being knighted. Never mind, take my advice -
get yourself a number one hit record - & you
cant go wrong.
       Good luck
       Izzy.

P.S. How about calling yourselves 'The Goodies' -
Nice one eh? - Dont forget - try to
appeal to the young folk - they're
more gullible.

( please send consultation fee by return)

       y X Izzy

# UNDER5

The *first* fab-mag for
"baby-boppers"

JULY 1974

## NAPPY CONTROL
on that very first date

## OVER THE HILL?
interview with Little
Jimmy Osmond

## IS MUMMY'S MILK FATTENING?
How to keep slim during
that difficult first year

## THE GRAND OLD MAN OF POP
Donny talks to Under5

## THE DISCO-NURSERY
a fab new idea

## THE GOODIES
exclusive

PLUS-Pics-fashion-
beauty-stories-letters

are you a GROOVY BABY?

# UNDER5 CONTENTS

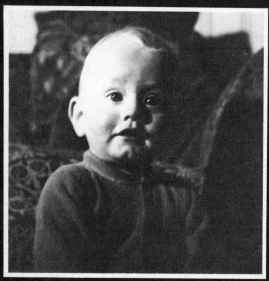

*This month's editor*

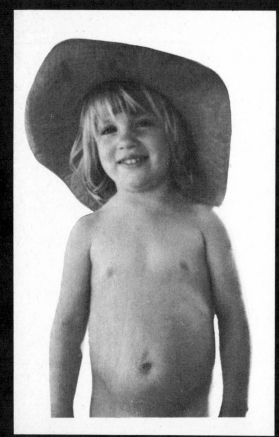

*Meet UNDER 5's playmate of the month*

## Acknowledgments

**Art direction:** Anthony Cohen

**Designed by:** Denis Hawkins, Rod & Kira Josey, Philip Bryden, Arnaldo Putzo, Kieran Stevens, David Ross, John Leach, Miguel Lopez Parras, Vicky Franklin, Martin Andrews and Prince Andrew.

**Photography by:** Geoff Goode, BBC Radio Times, Lynn News & Advertiser, Mary Evans Picture Library, International Photo Press, Evans Jones, M. Delanoe, Camera Press.

**With special thanks to:** Tom & Heloise Brooke, Linda and Alice, Danny, and Mrs Reader.

# Goodies!
## baddies more like

**by Annabelle Twee**

THE GOODIES could easily be the new rave on the baby-bopper scene this year. After rumours that they were splitting up, these veritable Chelsea Pensioners of Pop have reformed. Goody, goody! say I (*You* would; Ed.) Too old? "Not on your life" says slightly hunchbacked Tim Brooke Taylor, leaping from his bathchair. "How about Gary Glitter?" (How *about* him; Ed.) "He's sixty if he's a day, and I happen to know that's not his own hair". "Yes, I know that too" adds Bill Oddie, "We both get mowed at the same gardener". "The point is" (Graeme Garden speaking) "we are going to give the kiddiwinkies what they *really* want". "And that means lots of violence, kinky

clothes and naughty lyrics" says Bill. "And you should see our new act! We may be called the Goodies, but on stage we're anything but". And it's true . . . I've seen them and Wow! They have this great bit where they all come on as babies and chop up Alice Cooper; then Bill does some AMAZING things with a feeding bottle! And then . . . well, don't believe what you read – go and see for yourself! The Goodies are appearing at the One o'clock Club, Primrose Hill Kindergarten on Monday, and they have a guest spot on the "Woodentops" on Thurs. But . . . and how about *this? . . .* they've been BANNED from TOP OF THE POPS! Oh, AND they are working on a fab new rock stage show; "PIOUS XIV – SUPER POPE" . . . look out for *that.!*

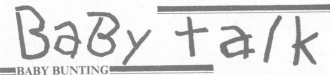

### ▬BABY BUNTING▬

Outrage stateside! LITTLE JIMMY OSMOND has upset millions of his fans by admitting that he is really 53 years old, a midget, and the FATHER of the so called brothers! . . . but GOOD NEWS for OSMONDS fans . . . from the Maternity Ward where a new OSMOND is expected any day now. The newcomer is set for College Dates as soon as he or she is weened, and he should make a British Tour next year, heading a bill that will include SLY STONE, DUKE ELLINGTON, YEHUDI MENUHIN, MARIA CALLAS, AND THE HALLE ORK . . . some show!
Grave news (ho ho) from NEW YORK, FRANK SINATRA died last week. He starts his fifteenth farewell tour in July . . .

TONY BLACKBURN has just entered Hospital for a head transplant. The donor is believed to be a SCOTS PINE.
Group news; EMERSON LAKE AND PALMER, following their recent split reformed to become LAKE PALMER AND EMERSON: they then split again but got together as PALMER EMERSON AND LAKE. Rumour hath it that there's still trouble . . . expect them to reappear as LEMERPAL AKER AND SON . . . LULU has split up . . . Round the Clubs: PETER NOONE is recovering from a nasty ordeal. Seems someone mistook him for a VENTRILOQUISTS DOLL and locked him in a suitcase for three weeks. On second thoughts, perhaps it was NO MISTAKE! Byeeeeeee!

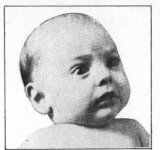 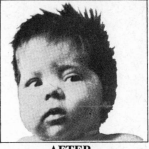

JANUARY 20 1974   No 7858   Price 10p

# THE SUNDAY TIMES

## Pious XIV, Superpope—a new musical

This tawdry little show (written and performed by Tim Brooke Taylor, Graeme Garden and Bill Oddie) gave me very little pleasure indeed. I found the acting embarrassing, the tunes forgettable and the dancing tedious. When one considers the basic subject matter, one can only lament an opportunity totally squandered. In vain I looked for spiritual dignity, historical veracity or a quick flash of pubic hair. At the final curtain I was so outraged that I was moved to sigh; and I fell off my surgical support and damaged my hearing aid, which only then did I discover had been mercifully switched off throughout. The audience loved it; and they loved the show too. No doubt it will run for years . . .

# British Lo

# ROLLING STONE

**ALBUM REVIEW**
**SUPER-POPE — SUPER TRIP**

Yeah, man, this is some heavy **** For a long time now these dudes have been threatening to get their **** together. Well, wait no more amigos, man, this is IT. What a mind blower! *****! It doesn't take a pretentious spaced-out head like me to spot the clue in the title. Super POPE . . . Dig the rhyme? POPE — DOPE . . . Right? THAT'S where it's at . . . and how! Whoooosh! ******* Far out, too much . . . like ****** . . . NICE . . . yeah . . . al RIGHT. . . . hmmmmmm . . . zzzzzzzzzz(SNORE) . . . threatening to get

# Melody Maker
FEBRUARY 9, 1974    9p weekly    USA 50 cents

| | | |
|---|---|---|
| 1 | (1) | **PIOUS XIV – SUPER-POPE (ORIGINAL CAST)** ...... The Goodies, Bent |
| 2 | (4) | **20 ORIGINAL HITS** The Session Singers, K Tel |
| 3 | (2) | **A TRIBUTE TO ELDRIDGE CLEAVER** The Black and White Minstrels, Bootleg |
| 4 | (7) | **MOTOWN CHARTBUSTERS VOL 237** Various Unknowns, Motown |
| 5 | (11) | **** **TO THE LOT OF YOU** John Lennon, Apple |
| 6 | (3) | **SLEEPALONGAMAX VOL 94** Max Bygones, Pye |
| 7 | (–) | **CLIFF'S DIRTY SONG BOOK** Cliff Richard, Rhubarb Tart |
| 8 | (6) | **THE LAST TRAM TO WIGAN** BBC Sound Effects Dept., BBC |
| 9 | (5) | **RIP YOUR KNICKERS OFF – I'M EVIL** The Osmonds, MGM |
| 10 | (–) | **THE YING TONG SONG ETC** Prince Charles, OBE |

# ALBUM OF THE MONTH

**PIOUS XIV SUPER POPE**
**(Original Cast)**
**Bent. Quintuple album**

This five record package represents nearly everything that is good about British Rock Music. Certainly, there are some flaws – sides five and nine are identical, and side seven has nothing on it at all – but there's more than enough good music on the other eight sides to keep the average fan happy for several minutes.

And what a range! It's ALL in here; echoes of Joan Baez, The Mothers of Invention, The Beatles, David Cassidy, Des O'Connor, Hendrix, Jimmy Osmond, Gilbert and Sullivan and The New York Dolls – and somehow, it works! Side two opens with a funky little thing sung by Joan of Arc (Tim Brooke Taylor) that sounds for all the world as if Moira Anderson is gigging with Grand Funk Railroad. Believe me, it's a complete gas. Other highlights include "Papal Blues", with some incredibly tasty guitar licks by "St Francis of Assissi" (Eric Clapton?) – in which "His Holiness" (Bill Oddie) gets off some of THE most poignant blues lyrics since Blind Lemon.

"I can bless you, I can damn you,
I can consecrate yo' soul.
But when it's Sat'day night at the Vat.
I just love to Rock and Roll."

Talk about telling it like it is! "Holy Ghost" is an amazing Moog freak-out that explodes into "Six Wise Virgins" with a bass riff that James Brown would be proud of; whilst "Cardinal's Crunch" is pure Slade — with "Wolsey" (Graeme Garden) doing a Noddy (top hat and all, I bet).

I could go on for hours; and the music does! The recording quality is excellent (remixed in Octophonic, at the thirty-two track studio in the Cistine Chapel, St Peter's, Rome) and the packaging is more than generous. The records come in a presentation gold casket, with forty-seven volumes of Belotti's "History of Catholicism" and a free-give-away original Michelangelo cartoon. Naturally with this kind of quality, it's not cheap, but if you're down to your last £546.17. here's how to spend it. You won't regret it.

Melody Maker
FEBRUARY 2, 1974
by weekly
USA 50 cents

THE Sun
FORWARD WITH THE PEOPLE
Monday, February 4, 1974

# LAND OF POPE AND GLORY

At last! A really good fun evening in the Theatre. And ... wait for it ... it's British! So let's give three hearty cheers!!! One each for the three stars of this all action-dancing-singing-rocking-rave up of a musical. "Wow! If the Vatican's really like this, I'll switch any day", said the Archbishop of Canterbury in the bar at the interval. And who was there on the stage doing the old knees-up with those pert and pretty Nuns in the finale?

You've guessed it – the old Archbish himself! It certainly brought the colour back to HIS cheeks; and it will to yours. So, go on, go and get an eyeful (and an earful) of the prancing prelate and the rest of the gang; you won't regret it. I was converted – and you'll be too; and I wouldn't mind betting my relics on that!

## Welcome to Bri

# A POPE-ULAR HIT!

Yes it's all here! Visions of Heaven (and what visions! the most nubile nuns *you've* ever seen), pageants of Purgatory, and the Fires of Hell. And when the temperature goes up, the trousers come down — it's THAT kind of show! Laughs, laughs all the way. The tunes are as infectious as a plague of boils; and the singing would rattle the walls of Jericho. Paradise regained? Blimey mate, I should say so!

Daily Mirror
EUROPE'S BIGGEST DAILY SALE
No. 21,786
Monday, February 4, 1974

**Izzy Bent Management Limited**
**Pop Agent**
**(Affiliated to The the Low Grade Organisation)**

My dear boys already,
 I am so happy for you - and _me_!
K_new_ you'd make it! What can I say -
except - here's my bill to date (enclosed)
Would appreciate payment by return post -
in used notes. Wouldn't want "anything
to happen to you".
 Love Izzy

THE GOODIES

Minutes of a <u>Special Emergency Meeting</u>

A special committee meeting was held under the Cricklewood Park bandstand at 9.45 on 28 July. Bill Oddie was in the chair, Graeme Garden was in the Gents, and Tim Brooke-Taylor was in tears. The treasurer was called upon to present his financial report, which is here reproduced.

<u>INCOME</u>

| | |
|---|---|
| 1½ million copies of "Super Pope" Album, personal appearances, etc. | £2,500,568.17p |
| Less Agents % | £1,900,234.02p |
| | £   56,960.30½p |
| Money owing to previous debtors on record account | |
| | £   56,960.30½p |
| Total due to <u>US</u> | |
| | £0,000,000.00p |

**FILE CLOSED**

# GOODIES SPLIT!

The wicked rat race of Rock and Roll claims three more victims. Despite selling one and a half million records in three weeks, The GOODIES have decided to split up. Bill Oddie, Musical Spokesman for the group, said: "The pressures of being a Super Group were just too heavy for us. Somehow the music was suffering. We've decided to cool it and just do our own thing for a while." Graeme Garden added: "This business is full of people who are "not very nice". I won't mention any names otherwise the "Boys" will be round to see us." Tim Brooke Taylor has started crying again . . .

panicles of red berries if you let it, is usu grown in gardens in its wonderful golden, leaved form *plumosa aurea*. One's object, this shrub, is to obtain the handsomest pos display of foliage, and to this end re pruning back of young wood should be p sed in the dormant season. I have n

now. In fact I've got thre like the one I was first duced to; I've got a simila but with a head that ligh that one seems to turn m friends on when they're us – and I've got a big one tha interchangeable heads. T

## STOP PRESS

**GOODIES REFORM**
**THE GOODIES** have re-signed for Decca records. A new Album will be released any minute now. Will they NEVER learn!?

scuss
rning
-ons"
make
ents
asure
ay be
t salt
s, as-
imul-
And
y be.
table
on.
lt is
as a
The
s not
tor's
the
tance
volve
e ex-

ising
n one
aped

THE QUEEN,
BUCKINGHAM PALACE
~~LONDON~~     away for ~~wares~~ SANDRINGHAM
                ~~try~~ ~~SANDRINGHAM~~
                      Norfolk.

No longer this address
    try          ~~Windsor Castle~~
                    ~~Middlesex~~

            on holiday,   try. "BRITTANIA"
                                THE PACIFIC OCEAN
        by
Buckingham Palace, London

TIM ♡←

LONDON
5 NOV

SANDRINGHAM
4PM
9 NOV
NORFOLK

WINDSOR
3PM
15 NOV
BERKS

LONDON
2AM
17 DEC
BUCKS

LONDON
4 AM
25 DEC

RETURN TO SENDER.

S.W.A.L.K.

# THE GOODIES
## No Fixed Abode, Nr. Cricklewood, Lon

~~Dear Missy Mrs Lis Elisa L Elise Eliss Elise Betty Queen MAd Majesty~~
~~Your majesty~~

Oh Queen,

        ~~Please can we have three O.B.E.s?~~
        Well, here we are in November again and, as we expect you know, it
is only fifty seven days to the New Year's Honours' List comes out.
~~Please can we have three O.B.E.s?~~ No doubt you have been thinking who
to ~~dish out the gongs to~~ honour, and have a few names in mind already -
lucky ~~sods~~ persons. You must be very busy and no doubt you sometimes
forget people who really OUGHT to have O.B.E.s ...like what you did
last year.
Anyway, just in case you're stuck - may we suggest ourselves?
We think we ought to have O.B.E.sbecause Tim looks very nice in a sash.
(See photo enclosed) Graeme is very clever and Bill will hit us if he's
left out.

Yours hopefully,

THE GOODIES

P.S. Can we have them before Christmas so we can hang them on the tree?
P.P.S. If you give one to Des O'Connor, Hughie Green, David Frost or
Jimmy Osmond, we'll send ours back.
P.P.P.S. If Charles fancies a part in one of our shows we will gladly
give him an audition.

P.P.P.P.S. Why dont you ever do a fullslength picture on the
stamps — I bet you've got smashing legs — B.?l.
P.P.P.P.P.S.   I shall be behind the pelican's feeding hut
in St. James' Park on Sat. at 5.00 clock — hint hint
                                        Tim X.

**Lois Comm and D. Nominator,**
**Chartered Accountants**

3 ?

The Goodies — Tax Relief in year ended April 1973̶4̶

Hello!

£      P

| | £ | P |
|---|---|---|
| Gross Income: | 28,431 | 73 |
| Tax Due on this amount: | 29,431 | 73 |
| Claims for Tax Relief: | 1̶8̶94 (3) | 73 |
| Support of a dependant (Tim) | 103 | 94 |
| "    "    "    (Graeme) | 103 | 94 |
| "    "    "    (Bill) | ½ cup of rice (value 103·94) | |
| Employment of Mrs. E. Tole (cleaner) | 13,437 | 08 (+ blackmail) |
| Clothes (Protective) | 7,930 | 43 |
| Hire of one six-legged Dromedary Skin | 155 | 00 |
| Japanese lunch | 10,000,071 | 31 (YEN) |
| Doctor's fees | 59 | 04 (IRISH YEN) |
| Accountant's fees for converting yen to sterling | 5,000 | 00 (YEN) |
| More accountant's fees | 28,431 | 73 |
| Rental of ½ hundredweight of fungus (assorted) | | 01 |
| Professional expenses | 29,431 | 73 |

43,000 14
43,000 18
29,431·73
17 231 26
43,000 17

**Total owed by Dept. of Inland Revenue
to The Goodies:**   23,431·73

Plus VAT
10%   £ **29,431·73** p

TOTAL: £ 7̶6̶,9̶6̶4̶ 00 p.

Signed:

*Lois Comm!*
*D. Nominator*

76,953·00 p.

well!

**Lois Comm and D. Nominator,**
**Chartered Accountants**

The Goodies — Tax year ended April 19~~72~~34 ³?

194 00
76 83½
25,193½

## INCOME

| | £ | |
|---|---|---|
| From : H.M. Government for hushing up Hovercraft scandal | 50,000 | 00½ |
| " : T.W. Stegendorf for supplying a hat | 32 | 03 |
| " : I.C.I. for discovering of synthetic petrol | NONE. | |
| " : Archbishop of Canterbury (for services rendered) | | 25 |
| " : Mummy on Tim's birthday | 76 | 83½ (Book Token) |
| " : "Loony" Jack Stremblie for laying lino | 194,000 | 00 |
| " : Oxfam | ½ cup of rice | (value 1.24p) |
| " : Ex-King Zog of Albania | | 2 only. |
| " : "A friend" for fixing the election     Total:- | $ 300 | 00 |

32.03
+ NONE
39.08

527.09
17) 24½
143
12
8 4
09

~~28,489~~ ~~54½~~
~~29,730~~ 29,431.73

## EXPENDITURE

| | £ | |
|---|---|---|
| money money money money | Rent, rates, light, heating, food. | | 8 | 37 |
| | Telephone | 3,017 | 24¼ |
| | Hire of 6-legged Dromedary Skin | 55 | 00 |
| | Magnifying glass and curly pipe    ✓6/10 Fair. | 21 | 53 |
| | Clothes (Protective) | 7,930 | 42 |
| money money money Money MONEY | Haircuts | NONE | |
| | Legal Fees | | 73 |
| | | 3,521 | 349 |

**MONEY!**

Fees for professional services to
Lois Comm, and D. Nominator:    ⟶   28,431 | 73 ✳

(Buy Heredes tomorrow)

Signed: Tim Brooke-Taylor xx
G.G. Bill Oddie.

Received with thanks Lois Comm.

TOTAL OWING:-   28,431 | 73 p

signed
Lois Comm.

# HOW TO BE

# A Bird-Watcher

# A SHORT BOOK BY Bill Oddie

# Chapter 1
# Why watch birds?

Why *not?* I resent this question. There's nothing *weird* about me, you know – I'm not a crank or something. I just happen to like watching birds, and that's THAT. And I don't want any of your silly remarks like "BIRD watcher oh yes? Eh Eh?" or "I'm a bit of a BIRD watcher too – TWO LEGGED variety . . . know what I mean?" Yes, ho ho, very funny. Well show me a bird that *hasn't* got two legs (unless of course you've chopped one of them off) I just happen to LIKE watching birds – do you MIND? Well, it's better than watching Yeti's or stones (which are quite boring and can't sing) or indeed Elephants (Cos Elephants can't fly so well). And a good thing too you say, I expect. Couldn't resist it could you? Well, that's a boring old joke. Almost as boring and old as "BIRD watcher eh eh?" So PACK IT IN and STOP GETTING AT ME. Or I shall CRY.

\*A "Wombat" has in fact four legs ; but most scientists would say a wombat is not a bird – and how right they would be.

# Chapter 2
# What do I need to watch birds with?

a) Eyes
b) A GOOD pair of binoculars. Or, If you're poor, a BAD pair of binoculars. These should be easy to handle, and NOT TOO HEAVY ; otherwise, when you put them round your neck, you'll fall over.

# Chapter 3
# What should I wear to watch birds in?

When you are poking round the countryside, peering in bushes through your binoculars, NEVER wear bright conspicuous clothes – you'll only draw attention to yourself and people will wonder what on earth you are doing. ALWAYS wear a dirty green floppy hat, a dirty green floppy anorak and dirty green floppy socks. I would also recommend a pair of waterproof pants – in case you see a rare bird and get over-excited. (Think about it . . .)

At all times it is essential that the birds do not see YOU. If they do, they will fall about laughing. You will then get upset.

It is therefore most important to find something in which you can completely secrete yourself when watching birds. Which brings us to HIDES.

# Chapter 4
# What is a hide?

Something in which you can completely secrete yourself when watching birds.

# Chapter 5
# How can I completely secrete myself when watching birds?

Get a HIDE, Dummy! Honestly! Questions questions! HERE are some different kinds of HIDES.

## A tree hide

### Disadvantages
It is impossible to reach your eyes with your binoculars when your arms are stuck down a hollow branch.

BEWARE OF Beavers, Woodpeckers, Dogs. (Also, in spring, when the sap is rising, beware of other trees).

## Wildfowlers Decoy

This should be very effective for getting really close to water birds. (I have not actually tried it myself. If anyone does have a go, please write and tell me if there are any disadvantages.)

## A Canvas Hide

### Disadvantages
When bird-watching on building-sites, this hide is easily mistaken for a temporary toilet.

Beware of Irish labourers after lunchbreak.

## 'Natural' Disguise

### Disadvantages
Fools nobody! Least of all a bird. But, just in case, don't try it in the mating season.

Waterproof Wellies.

# Chapter 6
# Where can I watch birds?

a) The Natural History Museum*
b) Trafalgar Square**
c) The Snowdon Aviary (London Zoo)***
d) Wild birds – not so easy. BUT . . . if you REALLY want to see lots and lots of really beautiful wild birds, find out where the government are going to build the next Airport or Power Station and go there – QUICKLY!

*Most of the birds here are, in fact, dead – but this makes it easier to watch them. Anyway, if you kick the glass case (when the attendant isn't looking) they do move . . . a bit . . . and you can PRETEND they are alive.

**Don't look up.

***Usually closed for repair. The birds do a lot of damage trying to get out of this big nasty cage.

# Chapter 7
# What do I do when I see a bird?

Blimey, you want to be told everything don't you? It's up to you what you do. Some people jump up and down, others roll on the floor giggling, others turn round and run away. You can stand on your head and sing Ave Maria for all I care.

If you really HAVE to be told . . . you should carry a note book and take detailed and accurate notes on where you saw the bird, when, the weather conditions, what it looked like etc etc. Here, for an example, is a typical page from my Bird Note Book.

# Chapter 8
# A typical page from my note book

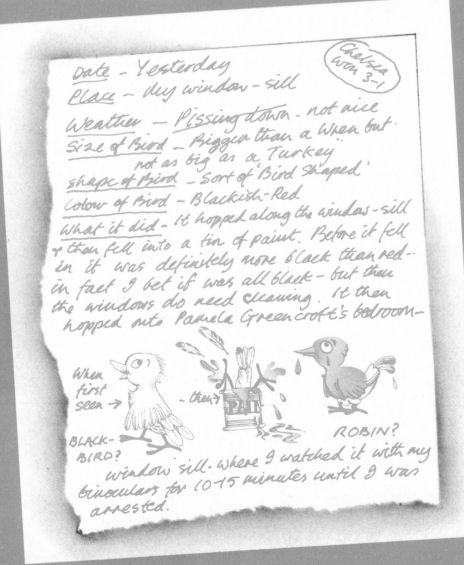

# Chapter 9
# An Introduction to bird identification

**A Duck** *

**A Lovable little Blue Tit** **

**An Owl (at night)** ***

**A Sainsbury's Chicken** ****

*Delicious – in bread sauce with an orange stuffed up its parson's nose.
** Not a full meal.
***If you enjoy the flavour of voles and shrews, this is most appetising. N.B. Make sure it is an owl and not a West Indian (not so tasty).
****Flightless.

# GOODIES'
# TOP SECRET FILE

**Title** *THE CASE OF*

*" THE ROYAL COMMAND "*

------

IF YOU SEE THIS FILE
**DESTROY IT**
★ IF YOU SEE THIS FILE ★

**EVER SO
EVER SO
SECRET**

ON SECOND THOUGHTS
YOU NEVER SAW IT ~

This must be burned.

# BUCKINGHAM PALACE, LONDON SW1, ENGLAND

Dear Goodies

I hope you do not mind me writing to you, but I am fed up, and I think you may be able to help. It's a long story but, well, here goes.

As you probably know, next Saturday is this year's Royal Variety Show (yawn yawn). Mum and Dad said I have got to go with them, but I said, I don't want to. I said, I don't like sitting through three hours of boring jugglers, and rotten Spanish ventriloquists and Des O'Connor and poncy posh ballet dancers. I mean, I <u>know</u> Mum and Dad <u>like</u> having jokes made about them and being bowed to and all that, 'cos it makes them feel wanted — but, well, all that 'variety' stuff may be OK for old folks (like <u>them</u>, tee hee) but it's not my scene. I asked Mum why she couldn't get The Slade or Sweet or Monty Python (rude bits and all!!). She said "Wash your mouth out!" and anyway none of them are signed to Lew Grade so they'd <u>never</u> be in it. So we had one heck of a stinking row. Well, to cut a long story short, they've said if I don't want to go, I needn't, but I shall jolly well be locked up in my room on Saturday night, <u>and</u> I've got to write out 100 times 'Max Bygraves is not a boring old fart'. <u>And</u> what's more they've cut my pocket money down to £2000 a week, <u>and</u> Dad says he's not going to buy me the Goons LP for Christmas after all.

So anyway — I've decided I shall jolly well have my Own Royal Variety Show — in My room (with 'tuck and pop!') Charles told me to write to the Goons but they can't come (actually Peter Sellers wanted too much money, Spike Milligan is away defending a daisy, and Harry Secombe is in the real Royal Variety Show — cheek! singing flippin' Welsh operas though, I bet, and not doing silly voices) and, well, Monty Python are a bit <u>past it</u> now aren't they? So I thought I'd ask you to come and do it.

Any chance?

Yours hopefully

Andrew

Andrew (Prince)

# THE GOODIES

## No Fixed Abode, Nr. Cricklewood, London

Wednesday 14th inst.

Dear Sir or Prince,

Thank you for your kind enquiry of the 12th inst.
We think we know the kind of thing that you have in mind and are pleased
to enclose our estimate for the proposed "entertainment".

Trusting that you will find our terms acceptable.

Yours,

*The Goodies*

THE GOODIES

---

<u>Alternative Royal Variety Performance</u>

<u>Estimate</u>

Time: 2 hours approximately

To hiring performers: Tim Brooke Taylor at £25 per hour............ £50
Graeme Garden at £25 per hour............ £50
Bill Oddie at 50p per hour............ £0I
To writing basic script.................................................... £0I
To hire of trandem ....................................................... £10
One falling over routine; 3 mins. at £6 per min. ........... £05
Funny business on bike; 2 mins. at £10 per min. .............. £18
Bill's song; 3 mins. at £0.05 per min. ...................... £20
To hiring custard pies, red noses, whoopee cushions,
revolving bow ties, six legged pantomime dromedary skin, etc. ..... £75

Total...................... £229.I5
plus V.A.T.

I0% deposit acceptable on acceptance of Estimate

---

## BUCKINGHAM PALACE, LONDON SW1, ENGLAND

Thursday I5th inst.

Dear Goodies

Thanks for your estimate - a bit steep, but - oh well - look, I'm
a bit short of the 'ready' right now - will you accept payment in
marbles, dead mice, OBE's, Crown Jewels, etc? Anticipating your
agreement I enclose a deposit of an orb and sceptre, a sash of the
Order of the Garter (slightly used), and a dead mouse.

See you 8.00 clock? Saturday

Yours

Andrew

PS - Mum and Dad will be livid if they find out what I'm up to.
Please try and slip in without anyone noticing. I enclose a plan
of the Palace.

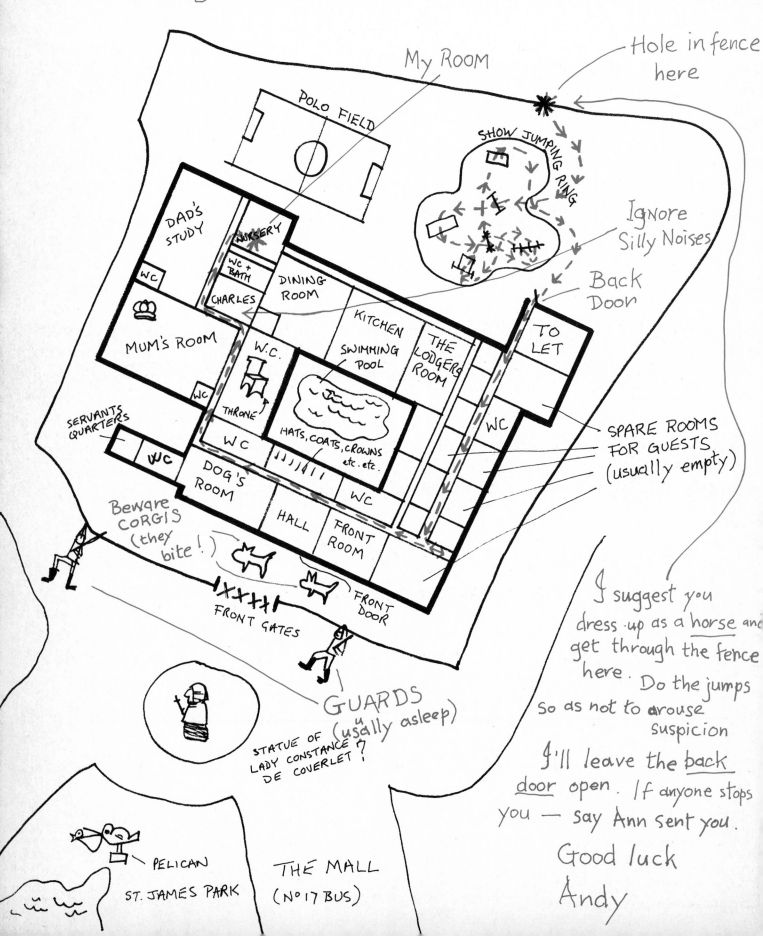

# ROYAL RUCTIONS

There were unprecedented scenes at the Royal Variety Show last night when the Royal Party walked out at half time, after giving the Black and White Minstrels the slow hand clap.

It just wasn't Her Majesty's night! For, returning home earlier than expected, she was struck in the face by a custard pie. It was believed to have been thrown by one of her sons (who prefers to remain anonymous) who was, he CLAIMS, defending himself from an onslaught of similar pies directed at him by "three unknown men". This story was later corroborated by the Prince's father, who did indeed catch sight of "three men" climbing over the palace railings. A slightly torn six legged pantomime dromedary skin was later found hanging from one of the spikes.

Later reports, from two Horseguards and a corgi, suggested that the three men ran off down the Mall carrying a sack. The sack is believed to contain twenty-five O.B.E.s, a small throne and most of the Crown Jewels.

The Prince was visibly affected by the incident and has only just stopped laughing. He is at present recovering on the Royal Yacht somewhere in the South Pacific and is unavailable for comment.

Police are anxious to establish the identity of the "three men". If caught, they could be charged with "High Treason"; if found guilty they will either be beheaded or incur a £5 fine.

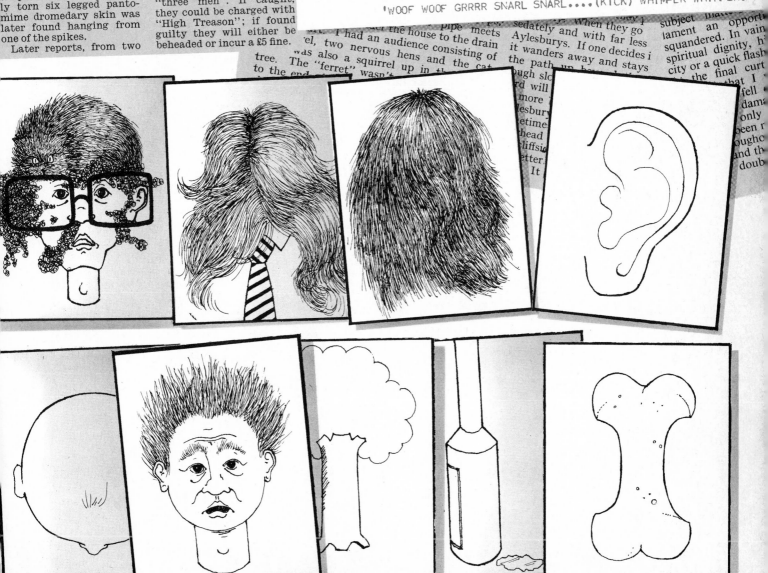

# METROPOLITAN POLICE
# WANTED
## FOR HIGH TREASON
## HAVE YOU SEEN THESE MEN

**REWARD: THREE FREE TICKETS TO NEXT YEAR'S ROYAL VARIETY SHOW —OR FIVE POUNDS IN PREMIUM BONDS, IF YOU CAN IDENTIFY THEM**

 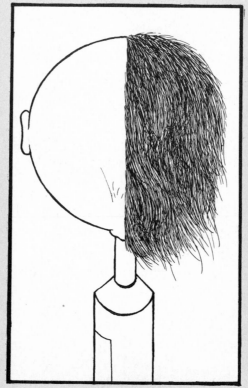 

ANY INFORMATION PLEASE TO: SUPERINTENDANT THUG, NEW SCOTLAND YARD

BUCKINGHAM PALACE, LONDON SW1, ENGLAND

Dear Super

The three men are called

THE GOODIES   and I claim my £5*

Yours Edward

* You can stuff the tickets !

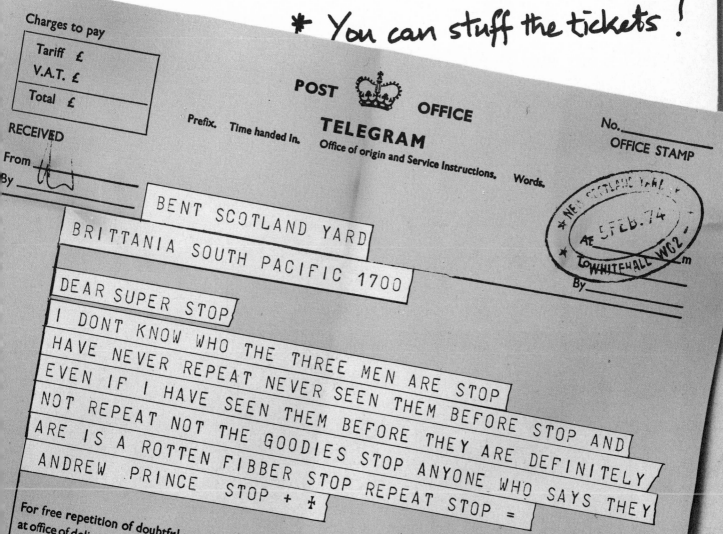

Prefix.   Time handed In.

POST OFFICE
TELEGRAM
Office of origin and Service Instructions.   Words.

No.
OFFICE STAMP

BENT SCOTLAND YARD

BRITTANIA SOUTH PACIFIC 1700

DEAR SUPER STOP
I DONT KNOW WHO THE THREE MEN ARE STOP AND
HAVE NEVER REPEAT NEVER SEEN THEM BEFORE STOP
EVEN IF I HAVE SEEN THEM BEFORE THEY ARE DEFINITELY
NOT REPEAT NOT THE GOODIES STOP ANYONE WHO SAYS THEY
ARE IS A ROTTEN FIBBER STOP REPEAT STOP =
ANDREW PRINCE STOP + +

For free repetition of doubtful words telephone "TELEGRAMS ENQUIRY"
at office of delivery. Other enquiries should be accompa...

all, nobody is going to look at an object of repulsion. Once she

# Police Baffled

Police are no nearer to establishing the identity of the "three men", after Prince Charles made a dramatic denial today. Scotland Yard have called in The Goodies to help them try and solve the case.

P.C. Bent has announced his retirement. He will now devote two days to writing a book entitled "Great Unsolved Mysteries of 1973" – to be serialized only in **this** paper!

*like to interview, like Salvador Dali and Mick Jagger, and sent it to the Editor of a very famous Fleet Street newspaper with a colour supplement. Unfortunately, poor old Angela hadn't done her homework properly. Yes, her list of famous people included two or three who were already deceased and interred.*

## Stop Press

### Goodies Find the Jewels

The missing crown jewels and the small throne were today returned to Buckingham Palace after The Goodies stumbled across them in a dustbin outside Buckingham Palace. A spokesman for The Goodies said: "I suppose someone must have thrown them out by mistake."

**Cup — 3rd Round**
**Half-Times**
Chelsea 7      Leeds 0
C. Palace   v   Rochdale
(declared No Contest)
Arsenal      Spurs
(retired hurt)

**Racing at Nonbury**
3.00 Entrecote Stakes
1. Queen's Stakes
2. Fancy Queen
3. Saucy Fuc

a nice tan but a bit sea-sick. Anyway. must close now. Thanks a lot, and remember — MUM'S THE WORD! eh?  Yours gratefully
A.

The Goodies
London.

# FILE CLOSED

# THE GOODIES
No Fixed Abode, Nr. Cricklewood, London

24th inst.

Dear Sir or Prince,

Nuff said! Our lips are sealed.

Yours ,
THE GOODIES

P.S. Hope no one missed the O.B.E.s!!

The Commissioner of Police
Metropolitan Division
London
Nr. Godalming
telephone 999

To:

Ch. Insp. G.W. Bottle,
F Div.,
G/936 - AA7.

*Friends in High Places ?!!!*
*E. J. (Mrs)*

My dear ~~Nancy,~~ George

May I begin by offering you my warmest congratulations on nailing the
East Acton Tuesday Sewing Circle and Terrorist Club - as nasty a bunch
of villains as ever drew pensions.  And of course a heartfelt "well
done!" for yet again winning the Lucky Spot Waltz at the Ball.  How <u>do</u>
you keep it up?

However, I'm afraid I must turn to graver matters.  It has regrettably
been brought to my notice that there is some concern over the recent
behaviour of one of your lads - and it may not surprise you to know I'm
speaking of P.C. Bent 362436.

Now we all know the sort of goings on that give us a bad name, but we're
men of the world - I'll always turn a blind eye to a little innocent
bribery (as long as the price is right) - but you know as well as I do
we can't allow a Copper to take the law into his own hands.  This Bent
lad has apparently started some sort of personal campaign against my old
friends the Goodies.  (As you will remember, they were very helpful to
us in the "Palace" case, since when they have enjoyed Police Protection
on the usual terms.)  We simply can't have constables carrying on like
Wyatt Earp and upsetting the system.  Apparently he has got himself mixed
up with some woman, and I needn't spell out what that can lead to. (Though
in your case, perhaps I do.)

I need hardly remind you that this letter is highly confidential, and
rather than trust the usual channels, I am giving it to my new cleaning
lady to deliver to you by hand.  (Incidentally, she came to me from the
Goodies with glowing references, so I know she can be trusted.)

The facts in this 'Bent' case are as follows:

P.C. Bent has recently purchased a curly pipe and violin, and has started
looking thoughtful (a bad sign in a copper).

The lad has been taking a lot of time off, but instead of drinking tea,
has been spending time in the Criminal Records Office.  Looking for
something?

Half a brick is missing from stores.

He was seen, only yesterday, in a heavy beard and long black wig, which
almost concealed his helmet, entering a shop in the West End run by
E.J. Beamont and Co., well known theatrical suppliers of 6-legged pantomime

P.T.O.

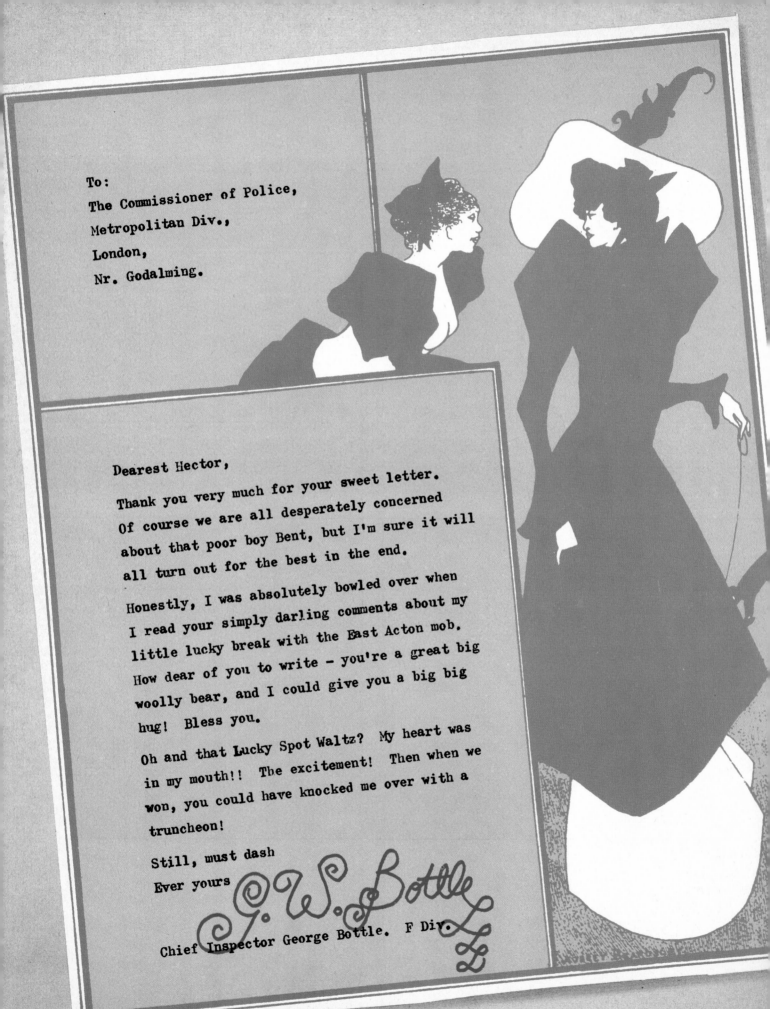

To:
The Commissioner of Police,
Metropolitan Div.,
London,
Nr. Godalming.

Dearest Hector,

Thank you very much for your sweet letter.
Of course we are all desperately concerned
about that poor boy Bent, but I'm sure it will
all turn out for the best in the end.

Honestly, I was absolutely bowled over when
I read your simply darling comments about my
little lucky break with the East Acton mob.
How dear of you to write - you're a great big
woolly bear, and I could give you a big big
hug!  Bless you.

Oh and that Lucky Spot Waltz?  My heart was
in my mouth!!  The excitement!  Then when we
won, you could have knocked me over with a
truncheon!

Still, must dash
Ever yours   *G. W. Bottle*

Chief Inspector George Bottle.  F Div.

# THE GOODIES' TRADITION

A Goodies' pamphlet

ropo.n.o.

# The Goodies Tradition

Early cave painting – Lascaux

"Throughout the ages there have always been men prepared to stand up and fight for what is right, proper, and good. Such men as these are *The Goodies*. Their essential spirit, and the spirit of those that came before them, has been captured by the world's greatest artists since the dawn of civilization, and often quite prettily. Anyway I think so. Jolly nice. Alright?"

*Sir Kenneth Clark*

recian Urn (by courtesy of
e British Museum.)

The Bayeux Tapestry (detail)

hIC EST TRANDEM          ET

Sketch by Leonardo da Vinci (pinched from Windsor Collection).

Hope dis·a da sorta ting
you want
Uv Pablo

# 300 Honours

# must be won

- ● **NO SKILL/TALENT REQUIRED**
- ● **FANTASTIC GIVE-AWAY OFFER**

## EVERYBODY'S DOING IT!

Footballers, Pop-singers, Disc-jockies – even Jazz musicians! These days, everybody – and ANYBODY – seems to have some kind of "Honour". So why should YOU be left out? There was a time when you had to have performed some great service to the nation like inviting princess Margaret to tea every other Sunday) but NOT ANY MORE. Now, at last, NEW YEAR'S HONOURS are to be made available to people like YOU. And what a difference it will make to YOUR life, if you get one.

## WHAT A DIFFERENCE!

We GUARANTEE that YOU will suddenly find out what it is like to be RESPECTED.

## SUDDENLY...

*Traffic Wardens will turn a blind eye when YOU park YOUR Rolls-Royce on the yellow line.
*YOU can razz up the M1 at *any speed you like!*
*Bank loans become *"No Problem".*
*Shopkeepers will knock "a bit off" at the merest whisper of those magic letters . . . O . . . B . . . E . . . !

## BUT DON'T TAKE OUR WORD FOR IT. FIND OUT FOR YOURSELF!

Why not take advantage of our special limited offer of a free PLASTIC REPLICA OBE? Sent, on approval, for two weeks, at absolutely no cost to YOURSELF. (Warning – on the 15th day the "OBE" will self-destruct, so PLEASE make sure YOU are not wearing it).

## OR ARE YOU ALREADY CONVINCED?

In that case, no need to bother with the plastic replica – just fill in the form and get THE REAL THING, by return of post.

## AND WHY STOP AT ONE?

There is NO LIMIT to the number of Honours YOU can possess (provided YOUR application is made through this advertisement). Make no mistake about it, the more letters YOU have after YOUR name, the more respect YOU'LL get – and the more YOUR friends will envy YOU!

Rules of the Competition:
No Cheating
Members of the Royal Family may not enter

YOUR CHOICE:
Silver, gold, re-inforced plastic or fibre glass.

FUNNY HAT
Free to every entrant

CHOICE
of fur, ermine, fox, gorilla, bandicoot or bushbaby.

*Plus* THESE INSTRUCTIONAL RECORDS

*How to talk Posh*

which will enable YOU to lose once and for all YOUR embarrassing local dialect, and replace it with a nice upper-class accent.

FEATURING:
the voices of: Analie Drummond-Hay, Lady Isobel Barnett, Brian Clough, and special "Mystery Guest".

AVAILABLE
with platform heels.

CHOICE OF COLOURS
Blue, red, prune or "poo-poo".

## DON'T DELAY–FILL THE FORM TO-DAY!

I THINK I OUGHT TO BE A KNIGHT/DAME/LORD/ OWNER OF AN OBE/MBE/ANYTHING ELSE/BECAUSE:

_____

_____

Signed:

Address:

I agree to abide by the rules of the competition*.
I do not already possess an Honour.
If I get an Honour, I agree to pay £10,000 per annum to the Royal Family Benevolent Fund (or the equivalent in champagne, horses, polo-mallets etc).
I enclose SAE and 50p postage and packing (75p for a Dukedom).
PLEASE ALSO SEND ME FREE MY COPY OF "THE QUEEN'S ENGLISH", PLUS INSTRUCTIONAL RECORDS "HOW TO TALK POSH", PLUS FREE FUNNY HAT. ☐ Tick for details of bookshelves

*OR*

PLEASE SEND ME EXPLODING PLASTIC REPLICA OBE ON 14 DAYS APPROVAL.
I realize that you accept no liability for damage/injury/death etc.

Signed:

Address:

Mrs E. Tole.
(Biographer - Researcher -
Informer - Snout.)

-
denfelt and Nickelson esq.

Dear Gents,
Well! The trouble I had to go
to to get this!! I know you wanted
what you called some juicy bits to
give the "File" a good ending, but
why I couldnt' just make up a pack
of lies I do not know. Anyway I
nicked this lot from Nancy Bottle'
Scrapbook, which was not easy
tell you. He came in just as
luckily mistook me for
pantomime dromeday.
I just hope you
worth it, and
one million

NOT TO BE TAKEN AWAY

# ...d Bailey Official Court Records

the case of

The Metropolitan Police v The so-called self styled clever-dick GOODIES

date 15th November 1974

Safely received, Stanley, petal. Bless you! x

George
Bottle of the Yard

N.B. This is THE official record of this case. There is one copy, and one copy only, and THIS is it. It is the PROPERTY OF THE OLD BAILEY CASE LIBRARY. The Library is open on TUES, WEDS and SATS (CLOSED AT HALF TERM, BANK HOLS AND IF CHELSEA ARE AT HOME) For REFERENCE only. The information herein is confidential, secret, and you shouldn't really be reading it.

Stan Ographer ........................(CLERK)

CLERK:

DAY ONE

It was a nice sunny morning when we all assembled in Number One Court. We watched Rod Laver beat Ken Rosewall in straight sets. Then we all moved to Number Two Court to get on with the case of THE METROPOLITAN POLICE V THE GOODIES. The judge was our very old friend Justice Once. At first he seemed overcome by the seriousness of the matter before him, and he was broody and silent. He then fell off his chair and was discovered to be, in fact, dead. A doctor confirmed that Justice Once had been in this condition for several months, but saw no reason why he should not continue with his duties. There was, however, an objection from the substitute bench, and the corpse was replaced by the first Pygmy Judge to sit on the Queens Bench (most of them are too little to reach). His name was Justice Ongat Wilite (laughter in court). The judge banged his gavel but the doctor applied a soothing ointment and he then introduced the case.

He explained that charges were to be brought against THE GOODIES by P.C. BENT of the Metropolitan Police. The Police case was to be conducted by the firm of BOOTS, BOOTS, BOOTS, BOOTS, MARCHINUP AND DOWNAGAIN (Solicitors). However, Mr. Boots was indisposed and had arranged that his place should be taken by Mr. Boots. Mr. Boots was, alas, rather nervous and was throwing up in the loo, and it was, therefore, agreed that Mr. Boots should deputise, until it was discovered that he was on holiday. The fourth Mr. Boots was apparently a typist's error, and Marchinup and Downagain were merely a silly joke thought up by the first Mr. Boots. The prosecution was eventually conducted by MR. IZZY BENT Q.C. (former theatrical agent, and no relation to P.C. BENT).

THE GOODIES asked for Legal Aid, but were told that it had all gone, and they had to make do with Lemon Aid. They elected to conduct their own defence, for reasons of poverty.

THE JURY were then selected, and consisted of MR. NATHANIEL BENT (CHAIRMAN), JEREMY AND ALOYSIUS BENT, THE BENT TWINS, COLONEL ARTHUR BENT, THE REVEREND PHYLLIS BENT AND THE FIVE "TUMBLING" BENT BROTHERS. (All no relations).

Each member of the Jury raised his right hand, and they were all allowed to leave the room.

MR. IZZY BENT (PROSECUTION) was then asked to name the charges brought against the so-called self-styled clever-dick GOODIES. MR. BENT consulted his client (MR. BENT). He then told the court that he couldn't really think of anything off hand, but he was fairly sure that THE GOODIES were likely to do something extremely naughty any minute. He appealed to the Judge to bring back hanging.

The Judge declared that he would adjourn the hearing for two days to give MR. BENT time to think up some really damning charges. He also appealed to the JURY to help MR. BENT think up something; and he appealed to THE GOODIES to do something criminal, which would, he said, make the case a lot easier.

COURT ADJOURNED

DAY TWO

Still thinking

## DAY THREE

This morning began with MR. BENT (PROSECUTING) bringing the following charges against THE GOODIES.

1: That they did issue a libellous statement against one MRS. E. TOLE, to wit; that: "This woman is a good for nothing old rat bag."

2: They did it again.

3: They might well do it yet again.

4: They are directly responsible for the rising cost of petrol.

5: They are directly responsible for the rising cost of everything else.

6: They masterminded the Watergate cover up.

7: They persuaded the BBC to do a second series of "FROST'S WEEKLY" (boos in court).

8: They started the French Revolution.

9: They discovered America.

The Judge reminded MR. BENT that all these allegations must be proved BEYOND ALL REASONABLE DOUBT. After consulting his client, MR. BENT decided to withdraw the last six charges.

THE GOODIES pleaded GUILTY to the charges of libel, repeated libel and intended repeated libel, but claimed it was FAIR COMMENT.

MR. BROOKE TAYLOR assured the court that he would call many witnesses who would testify to the good name of THE GOODIES. These would include SHEIK AHMED EL FATA, MR. EDWARD HEATH, MR. RICHARD NIXON, MR. DAVID FROST, CARDINAL RICHELIEU and CHRISTOPHER COLUMBUS.

At this point the Judge asked THE GOODIES if they had a criminal record. They replied (not surprisingly) that they indeed possessed an LP of LITTLE JIMMY OSMOND. It was played. MR. OSMOND was sentenced to ten years hard labour (ON THE MAX BYGRAVES SHOW).

                                        COURT ADJOURNED

## DAY FOUR

### THE PROSECUTION

MR. BENT today opened his case. He took out his sandwiches, and closed it again. He then asked MRS. E. TOLE to take the witness box. She did so, but the Judge made her put it back. MR. BENT then began his cross-examination of MRS. TOLE, which is here transcribed in full.

| | |
|---|---|
| BENT: | Your name is MRS. EDNA TOLE. |
| MRS. TOLE: | Yes, I know it is. |
| BENT: | Would you please tell the court, Mrs. Tole, are you a good for nothing old rat bag? |
| MRS. TOLE: | Yes. (Laughter in court). |
| BENT: | (Very slowly) I am going to ask you that question again, and this time I want you to think very carefully, and take as long as you like before answering. Are you, Mrs. Tole, a good for nothing old rat bag? |

                                        COURT ADJOURNED

| | |
|---|---|
| MRS. TOLE: | ...... Yes. |
| BENT: | I'm sorry M'Lord but I've forgotten the question. |
| JUDGE: | I think Mrs. Tole meant to say "No" ... Is that right Mrs. Tole? |
| MRS. TOLE: | Yes. |
| BENT: | So! You deny it? |
| MRS. TOLE: | Yes. |
| BENT: | And would you tell the court please what you, in fact, ARE? |
| MRS. TOLE: | Yes. |
| BENT: | WHAT are you? |
| MRS. TOLE: | I am a good for nothing old rat bag. |
| BENT: | You see M'Lord she answers with a modesty that surely testifies to her excellence of character; and how these nasty foul-mouthed, so-called GOODIES could libel her so wickedly, I do not know! |
| MR. BROOKE TAYLOR: | But M'Lord Mrs. Tole has just admitted that she is indeed a good for nothing old rat bag. |
| BENT: | She is also a dotty old crone who doesn't know what she's talking about and I submit, M'Lord, that her testimony is totally untrustworthy. |
| JUDGE: | I agree. Mrs. Tole strikes me as a loony. |
| MRS. TOLE: | Thank you sir. |

SO ENDED THE CASE FOR THE PROSECUTION

COURT ADJOURNED

## DAY EIGHT

### THE DEFENCE

MR. BROOKE TAYLOR (DEFENDING) today began his defence of the defendants.

| | |
|---|---|
| MR. BROOKE TAYLOR: | M'Lud I shall now prove that, on the night in question, myself and my colleagues were, in fact, at a "party" in the private rooms of a gent of some public standing, and, what's more, you can't touch us for it. I call my first witness: Chief Inspector George Bottle. |
| MR. BROOKE TAYLOR: | You are Chief Inspector George Bottle, and you are, I believe, also known as "Nancy". |
| BOTTLE: | Takes one to know one, chubbycheeks. |
| MR. BROOKE TAYLOR: | Nancy ... would you tell us please what you were doing on the night in question? |

| | |
|---|---|
| BOTTLE: | Well YOU should know that, sweetie pie ... <u>wasn't</u> it fun? |
| JUDGE: | Will you please answer the question Mr. Bottle? |
| BOTTLE: | Oh come on, I don't have to tell YOU, Sugardrawers... you can't have forgotten <u>already</u>! |
| BENT: | Are you implying that his Lordship was present at this "party"? |
| BOTTLE: | Well <u>you</u> saw him, didn't you? |
| BENT: | Er... that is for the Jury to decide. |
| JURY: | We saw him! |
| MR. BROOKE TAYLOR: | Quite a party wasn't it? |
| ALL: | Yes! |
| MR. BROOKE TAYLOR: | Now, I put it to you, Mr. Bottle, that certain <u>other</u> people were also present at this "party", whom, for reasons of security, I shall refer to as Mr. A, Mr. B, Sheik C, The Right Honorable D, President E, Cardinal F, Mr. G, Sir H, and Tortoise I.  Is that correct? |
| BOTTLE: | Almost, petal. In fact Mr. B was out burying his granny, but Mister K, L and M were there too, and so was Mr. or Mrs. N ... I'm STILL not sure about him, are you?... anyway ... oh yes, and the Tortoise was X, not I. |
| MR. BROOKE TAYLOR: | And I believe certain photographs were taken of these certain people? |
| BOTTLE: | I should say SO, cheeky chops! |
| | THE CERTAIN PHOTOGRAPHS WERE THEN PASSED ROUND THE COURT.  THEY ARE HERE ATTACHED. |

DAY NINE

STILL LOOKING AT PHOTOGRAPHS

DAY TEN AND ELEVEN

STILL LOOKING

DAY TWELVE

The day began with the Court in uproar as MR. BROOKE TAYLOR called his key witnesses; MISTERS A, G and K, SHEIK C, THE RIGHT HON. D, PRESIDENT E and CARDINAL F.  So that their faces should not be recognised, they appeared in the guise of a six-legged Pantomime Dromedary, who was then cross examined thus:

| | |
|---|---|
| MR. BROOKE TAYLOR: | You are Misters A, G, K, Sheik C, The Right Honorable D, President E and Cardinal F? |
| DROMEDARY: | Yes. |
| MR. BROOKE TAYLOR: | Could you tell the court, do you see anyone here today whom you would describe as a good for nothing old rat bag? |
| DROMEDARY: | Yes. |

MR. BROOKE TAYLOR:   Would you point to that person, please?

The Dromedary then pointed to the Judge, two members of the Jury, Chief Inspector Bottle, and - crucial evidence, this - MRS. E. TOLE.  In doing so, the animal occupied five of its six legs, and fell over.  THE GOODIES helped it up.

DROMEDARY:              Thank you.  And whilst I'm at it, I would also like
                        to thank you, and your colleagues, for negotiating my
                        oil deal, for trying to work out my anti-inflationary
                        policy, for editing my tape, for getting me another
                        series, for defeating the Huguenots and for piloting the
                        Santa Maria.

GOODIES:                Lies, all lies!

                                            COURT ADJOURNED

DAY THIRTEEN

THE VERDICT

THE JURY FOUND THE GOODIES "GUILTY" ON ALL NINE CHARGES.

THE SENTENCES

JUDGE:                  Goodies, I am sure you <u>are</u>, in fact, guilty of this
                        libellous statement against MRS. TOLE, but then so is
                        everyone else, so it doesn't count.

                            Also, though you are apparently guilty of the
                        other six charges, MR. BENT saw fit to withdraw them
                        on the first day, so they don't count either.  Therefore,
                        I cannot pass sentence on you, which is a pity because
                        I am in an ingenious mood and I had thought up some very
                        amusing punishments ... never mind.

                            Finally, I would like to remind everyone in this
                        courtroom that what you have heard during the past
                        thirteen days is of the upmost secrecy.  Some of the
                        revelations uncovered during this hearing have been to
                        say the least, sensational.

                            I fully realise that some sneaky, unprincipled,
                        enterprising publishers could very easily make a great
                        deal of money if they got their hands on some of this
                        fascinating information.

                        (CRIES OF "SHAME", "HOW <u>COULD</u> THEY" AND "OVER MY DEAD
                         BODY")

                            If this does happen ... I shall be extremely cross ...
                        if I do not get my usual rake off.  The case is now
                        closed.

BOTTLE:                 May I have my photos back?

JUDGE:                  No.

                                            COURT ADJOURNED

                                        *Stan Ographer* (CLERK)
                                        Feb. 1974.

# THE
# SNOOCHIE
# KOOCHIE
# CLUB

### GRAVESEND

To:

Weidenfeld & Nicolson,
"Publishers",
Room 13a,
The Hostel,
Penge.

Dear Sirs,

    I regret that I must inform you that it has come
to our notice that you intend to publish material
defamatory to certain parties known to us as
"The Goodies."

    Well, you can take it from me, hearts, any attempt on
your part to make public these documents, as supplied by
Mrs. Edna Tole (Mrs) and Sherlock Probert Ltd (formerly
ex-police constable Bent) will result in prosecution, and
the possibility of some big coppers coming round your place
to interview you over the head with half a brick.

    So be told!

    All the best,

*G. W. Bottle*

        Chief Insp. G.W. Bottle
        Metrolopitan Police.

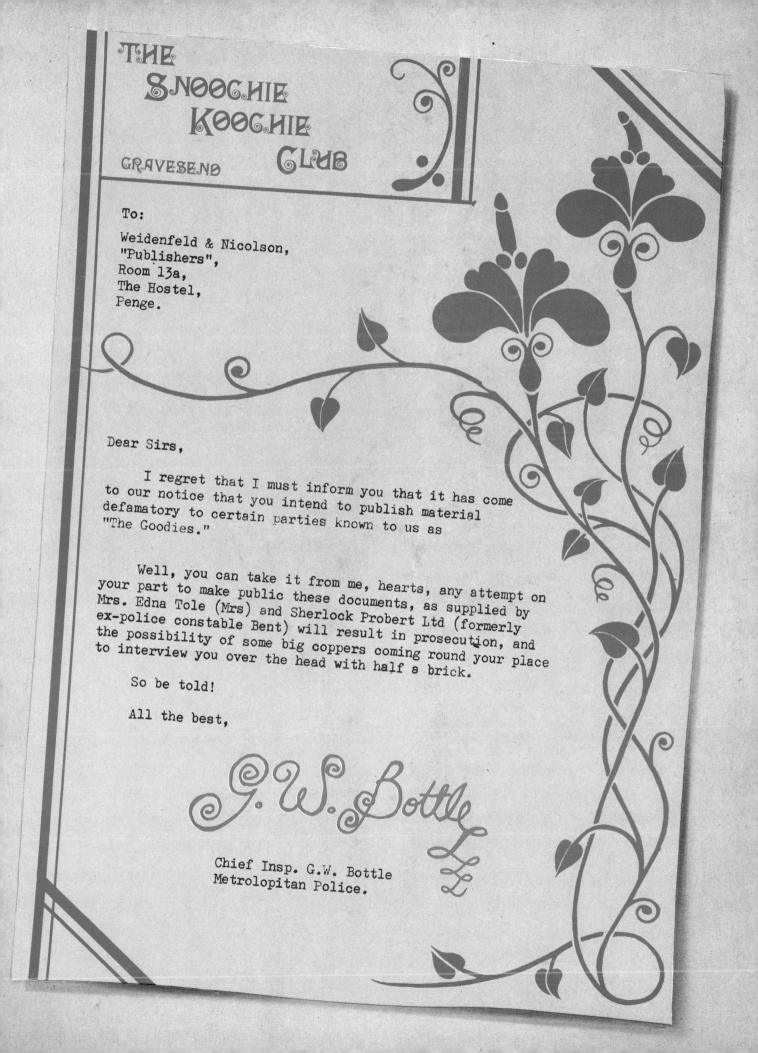

George Weidenfeld and Nicolson Limited

# Weidenfeld & Nicolson

*now at :* The Alhambra Theatre Nr. Small Widdlington Parva Kansas City Somerset  *Telephone* 01-228 8888

*Registered, number* 395166 England  *Telegrams and cables* Nicobar London SW11 1XA  *Telex* 918066

```
to: Chief Inspector "Nancy" Bottle,              Today.
    c/o the Metrolopitan Police,
    (or try 'Cecil's' in Brewer St.,)
    LONDON
    ENGLAND
    Nr France.
```

Dear Chief Inspector Bottle,

We were deeply concerned to receive your recent communication regarding our intended publication of "The Goodies File".

Of course we had not realised the severe implications of our actions, such as the big policemen coming round our place etc.

We can only reassure you that, in view of these circumstances, we shall of course go no further with this venture.
Moreover we dissociate ourselves totally from the dubious activities of Mrs Edna Tole (Mrs) and ex-P.c. Bent (Now Gladys and Partner, amazing stunts with a Combine Harvester, and a great success too we might add!) Our only defence in the circumstances is that we were prepared to accept P.c. Bent's evidence as reliable, as his father, Hector Bent, is an old friend of ours, and I gather carries some weight in your organisation.

It now appears we have been sadly deceived, and wishing no harm to come to your colleagues The Goodies, we give you our solemn word that we have no intention of publishing the aforementioned work. *This is true.*
*(Legal Dept.)*

Furthermore, we promise not to publish it.

In conclusion, it is definitely not our intention to publish the facts made known to us.

Even if we did publish them, we probably wouldn't make the money we expected anyway. So we won't. Promise.

Honestly, we aren't going to publish the Goodies File.

Really and truly.

So there it is. We must meet for a drink sometime.

Yours

*P. T. O.*

*Chairman and Joint Managing Director* Sir George Weidenfeld
*Deputy Chairman* John Weidenfeld  *Joint Managing Director* Steven Weidenfeld  *Assistant Managing Director and Company Secretary* David Frost
*Directors* Stewart Weidenfeld  Mavis Weidenfeld  Jim Weidenfeld  Jeremy Weidenfeld (deceased)
Michael Weidenfeld  Bill Weidenfeld  Fingers Weidenfeld  Doreen Weidenfeld  Nigel Weidenfeld  Ethel Weidenfeld

Cheers!
Weiden Feld & Nicholson

Weiden, Feld, and Nicholson.
"A song, a smile, and amazing stunts with a grapefruit."

Currently at the Alhambra, Stoke

**BRITISH ARMY INTELLIGENCE**
"Dunpeepin"
Edgbaston
Nr. Omsk

19.10.74

Dear Mrs Tole,

I am returning the enclosed Dossier on 'The Goodies' which you so kindly sent, as I am afraid it is of no immediate interest to us. Nor indeed could we consider paying you the sum of one million pounds that you mention, although we do appreciate your remarks on the current price of butter.

Suggest you try elsewhere — the Chinese might be interested.

Regards

*Major Eyes-Water*

Major Eyes-Water

CONFIDENTIAL

HANDS OFF!!

NO NO NO!

Sorry – no use to us
Admiral T. Arch
Naval Intelligence

Return to sender.
M Suggs (Mr.)

Lord off Rubbish!
Wingko Zeppelin
RAF Spying Dept.

East Peter Secret Polise.

Oh come on!
Elizabeth R

Dear Mrs Tole

Try News of the World
yours Sunday People.

Try Sunday People
Yrs. News of the World

You're just tried us
ys. Sunday People.

Well don't send it back to us

No thankyou
auntie.
love to uncle Bop
Ethel E Stan x

N.O.W.

Might just be something
here I could use.
Bless you !!!
D. Frost.